# HOMEOWNER ASSOCIATIONS

# HOMEOWNER ASSOCIATIONS

*What you should know before buying in an HOA,
and how to become an effective HOA member.*

## C. J. Klug

iUniverse, Inc.
New York   Bloomington

**Homeowner Associations**
**What You Should Know Before Buying in an HOA**
**and How to Become an Effective HOA Member**

iUniverse books may be ordered through booksellers or by contacting:

iUniverse
1663 Liberty Drive
Bloomington, IN 47403
www.iuniverse.com
1-800-Authors (1-800-288-4677)

Because of the dynamic nature of the Internet, any Web addresses or links contained in this book may have changed since publication and may no longer be valid. The views expressed in this work are solely those of the author and do not necessarily reflect the views of the publisher, and the publisher hereby disclaims any responsibility for them.

ISBN: 978-1-4502-5840-1 (sc)
ISBN: 978-1-4502-5842-5 (hc)
ISBN: 978-1-4502-5841-8 (ebk)

Printed in the United States of America

iUniverse rev. date: 09/29/2010

This book is dedicated to the volunteer homeowners who give of their time and energy to serve on their HOA Boards of Directors. These individuals rarely receive the recognition and appreciation deserved, although their communities could not operate or prosper without them. I was fortunate to have worked with several outstanding HOA Boards of Directors for Palm Desert Greens, Nellie Gail Ranch, Niguel Shores and Coto de Caza.

I also would like to express my personal appreciation to the on-site manager HOA/POA members who former the Community Manager International Association. Their professionalism, friendship and annual workshops make us all better managers.

# Preface

The purchase of a home is probably one of the most important decisions most people ever make and being in a Homeowners Association (HOA) may be a significant consideration. As an on-site manager for over 25 years, I have found that most buyers do not recognize that Homeowner Associations are contractual relationships and before buying property within an HOA the recorded documents should be carefully read and understood. Most often, with the volume and complex paper work of the escrow, title documents, disclosures and financing, the recorded HOA's Conditions, Covenants, and Restrictions (CC&Rs) are not thoroughly understood, if read at all. The purpose of this book is to provide information on Homeowner Associations, their benefits and possible pitfalls. This book contains two sections, the first summarizing what an HOA is and how or why they exist; with the second section being a collection of responses to questions from homeowners on a variety of related subjects that may be experienced with HOA property ownership.

******

# CONTENTS

## PART 2
## RESPONSE TO QUESTIONS

Opinions expressed are generalized and are not intended to be a substitution for consulting with appropriate legal counsel or other professional advisors. Also specific association documents, local state statutes, or the timing of the question could result in a different answer.

# HOMEOWNER ASSOCIATIONS
*What you should know before buying in an HOA,*
*and how to become an effective HOA member.*

## By C. J. Klug

## WHAT IS AN HOA

Home ownership in the past few years has undergone a lot of changes where owners have desired shared amenities, maintenance of common areas and enforcement of neighborhood standards, while at the same time government has been reluctant to assume such responsibilities. In some States, it is estimated that close to 20% of homes are now located in Homeowner Associations. The expectations are that the growth of homes in Homeowner Associations will continue because many local governments do not want to take on the financial liability of new streets, parks, landscaping, etc. due to budget concerns. These communities with shared common area facilities are generally referred to as a Common Interest Development (CID) and need a managing entity, a Homeowners Association (HOA), which may sometimes be referred to as a Property Owners or Community Association. As a property owner in an Association you are automatically a member of the association of owners which is in charge of operating and maintaining the common area and services to its members. As a member, you must also share in the expenses by paying regular assessments to the Association.

An HOA is generally a private, Non-profit Mutual Benefit Corporation in which all property owners automatically are members when property is purchased and will have certain rights and obligations. An Association does not have to be incorporated, but from a legal and liability standpoint it is strongly recommended.

The Association runs things as a sort of mini-government, operating under the Covenants, Conditions and Restrictions (CC&Rs), originally established by the developer, and in some areas with additional regulations set by State Law. In an Association the majority rules and what the group wants, within parameters of the recorded documents, you have to accept or convince the group to change. The Association's automatic membership should not be confused with a voluntary civic or social club where you can "quit". As long as you own your property you are a member. An Association may only consist of a few units that share common walls or a driveway, or can be several thousand homes with private streets, clubhouses, hundreds of acres of common area landscaping and a variety of recreational facilities.

Your interests as a homeowner are in concert with the continuing success of the Association. If the Association functions well, the lifestyle you have moved there for and your property values will be maintained or enhanced. If the Association is not well run, common area not well maintained or the community does not have a good reputation, property values may be lower. In large developments, a homeowner may be required to be a member of more than one Association. When there is a Master Association it may be responsible for over all facilities such as streets, gates, clubhouses and general rules enforcements, and then there may be Sub-Associations for areas or types of buildings with special services, such as exterior painting. Each Association would have its own Board that adopts a separate budget and assessments. Common Interest Developments were initially promoted as offering "care free living", and although many aspects of home ownership are taken care of by the Homeowners Association, there are substituted responsibilities of paying assessments and participating in managing the Association.

## IS AN HOA THE RIGHT DECISION

Buying in a development with a Homeowner Association is a personal and economic decision with no simple answer as to if it is a good or bad decision. Often the buyers' desire for a particular style of house, view or other amenity is only available in a development that is in an HOA and thus does not leave a choice. Developers create HOAs in order to offer amenities to attract buyers or in some cases because it is necessary to get City or County approval to develop the property. Large resort communities continue to gain in popularity by offering recreation, maintenance services, and security to a wide variety of homeowners at affordable prices. Retirement Communities for active seniors are also growing in popularity as the American population ages.

Following is an abbreviated list of factors to be considered when buying in an HOA:

### DESIRABLE AMENITIES/SERVICES

The first question is what services are desired with your home or investment property? Do you want access to such things as golf or tennis, heated swimming pools, clubhouse or someone else responsible for exterior maintenance? Is a restricted community access gate desired for added security? Will you be satisfied having someone else deciding on the type and level of care for landscaping and exterior painting? Will you like a more structured environment established by others for both property maintenance and personal behavior rules?

### IS THE HOA COST WORTH IT

How much are you willing to pay for having services or recreational facilities? How do you feel about paying for facilities that you do not use? Can you financially handle increases in monthly costs that may be assessed by the governing Board or result from decisions by a majority of homeowners with which you may not agree? Often homeowners are unrealistic about maintenance costs and feel they can do things much cheaper themselves, which will not be an option in an HOA. How will you feel when you no longer use facilities, perhaps due to health or other problems, but will still be a shared cost to you? Second home owners or vacationers generally appreciate having things taken care of when they are away. There is also a benefit in having the HOA deal with obtaining bids, contractors, insurance and complying with governmental regulations.

## PERSONAL PARTICIPATION

Will you like participating in governing your HOA? Although your participation may only consist of paying assessments and voting on issues presented to the members, it will be important to the success of the HOA. Would you like the opportunity to participate with your neighbors on how the HOA operates by volunteering to serve on Committees or the Board of Directors? HOAs can be much like the Townhall Meetings of the original New England Communities where residents gathered to discuss common problems and to agree upon solutions and community standards.

## PETS, PARKING & PARTIES

The most common complaints and rules enforcement problems in Associations usually involve loose pets, parking enforcement and loud parties. Because it is private property, animal control or police will not enforce rules or patrol, but only respond to formal disturbing the peace or criminal complaints. Large Associations may have paid personnel or contract with private security for enforcement, but members may need to become more involved with formal complaints. Guests are often the most frequent violators as the Association lacks authority to levy fines against them since they are not members of the

HOA. The owner that authorized their entry may be held responsible for violation fines if the owner can be identified. Towing is the best parking violation control, but has strict posting requirements plus having a contract with a licensed towing company.

## FINANCING

The HOA monthly assessment may reduce the maximum loan that can be obtained because the Association assessment will reduce your calculated available monthly income that determines your maximum payment the lender will allow. On the positive side, some homebuyers, not in an HOA, do not allow a reasonable amount for property maintenance that in the long run could result in the decline in the property's curb appeal and lower values for the general area. An HOA can establish a budget and provide a minimum standard of maintenance for all properties from funds collected monthly from all owners. Lenders may be more comfortable with lending in a community with guaranteed maintenance where there are adequate Reserve funds for major repairs and replacements.

## MAY NOT HAVE THE OPTION

If a home is desired in areas where the only single family units are in multistory buildings there may not be a choice about being part of an HOA, since there must be an entity to manage and maintain the structure and common areas. Multistory buildings will by necessity have complex documents to define who has liability at risk and responsibility for maintenance and repairs. Buyers should have a clear understanding as to where the resident's responsibility starts for plumbing, electrical and walls, and know where the personal property joins the common area pipes or wiring and thus who will bear the costs for any repair or maintenance. Some buildings are Cooperatives, where the Association will maintain all major fixtures and appliances, and thus have greater authority and costs.

## HOA FINANCIAL STABILITY

When there is a desire to live in a Common Interest Development (CID) that maintains the living structure or significant special amenities, the HOA should be researched to determine if there is a history of effective management and fiscal stability. Are there adequate reserves and cash flow to handle capital replacements or unanticipated repairs? What is the Association's budget and assessment rate history? Assessment rates with irregular increases should be carefully reviewed. Determine how often there have been Special Assessments and their purpose, which could be an indication of poor fiscal management. Lenders will also look at the financial condition of the HOA, particularly Reserves available and the number and amount of delinquent accounts.

## INVESTMENT/RENTALS

Investors and landlords usually appreciate having fewer items to deal with such as exterior maintenance, pools, etc., although the owner does still have the ultimate responsibility for uncorrected violations. Because the HOA contract is with the property owner and not the tenant, fines for any violations of the Associations rules will be assessed against and be the responsibility of the property owner, who may have to collect from the tenant.

## OWNER/RENTER RATIO

The percentage of owner occupied units compared to rentals is an important factor for most communities. Resident owners will take a greater interest in the management and condition of the community and lending may be negatively impacted by a high percentage of rentals. HOA rules should also be verified as to the minimum length of rental periods. Rental length may not be regulated or may require minimums of six months, 30 days or in the extreme, permit daily rentals. Obviously short term rentals or time share units can change the character of the development. Associations may also have additional fees or deposits for tenants. In some Associations the owner must transfer their use and access rights to facilities to their tenants when their units are rented.

## ARCHITECTURAL CONTROLS

Most HOAs have architectural regulations with review committees that control all exterior modifications. The approval process can be time consuming and owners may feel it infringes on their property rights. Although the CC&Rs will describe the process, often the final decision may be quite subjective. The benefits of architectural control are that the quality of improvements and the character of the community will be maintained. In many HOAs, neighbors may receive hearing notices and thus have an increased influence in the approval or modification conditions for exterior improvements.

## DENSITY

Many HOAs were created to permit a higher density and thus the units may have less privacy and closer contact with neighbors. Thus some units will never be able to be expanded. In some cases this is an advantage because there is less area to be maintained and there are more units to share in the costs of Association amenities and services. Shared entries can be uncomfortable for owners who are accustomed to more individuality and privacy. There may also be less storage areas available.

## LOWER UNIT COST

Higher densities and shared amenities in some cases are to make the units cheaper and thus result in lower unit costs with lower down payments. Higher density may also result in lower maintenance costs on a continuing basis. However the lower entry cost and reduced loan payments may be offset by the Association's monthly assessment payments.

## LITIGATION HISTORY

Buyers should verify that there are no significant pending law suits involving the Association that could result in future special assessments. Also check the past litigation history and basis for the suits. In the 80s and 90s there were a rash of defect construction law suits against HOA developers that curtailed many CID projects, but State law changes appear to have lessened the problem. Law suits can also be an indication of community conflict and instability. Some areas of the country have more litigation problems in general.

## SPECIAL ASSESSMENTS

Always check if there are any current or pending special assessments and their justifications. Although there may be good reasons for a special assessment, it can be an indication of poor financial management or structural problems. Unexpected large special assessments could cause financial hardships for fixed income owners.

## IS DEVELOPMENT COMPLETE

If a development is complete the quality and stability of the project and individual home values can reasonably be evaluated. If the developer is still active there may be concerns that the type of units, density or construction quality could change and affect property values of existing units. Also recreational facilities may not be adequate when more units are occupied. The developer may also be subsidizing the Association's maintenance budget to facilitate sales, and fees or quality of services may change when the developer leaves. Early purchasers may benefit from a lower price because as sales become stronger prices are usually increased. If sales are weak, prices will normally not be lowered but rather incentives given to new buyers through decorator upgrades or lower financing costs.

## APARTMENT CONVERSIONS

During real estate boom periods, there often are apartment buildings that are converted to condominiums. These units should be carefully evaluated because they may appear modern with new appliances, floor coverings and décor, but the building is still much older. Also apartment building were generally not built to as high a standard of noise suppression and quality construction as new buildings, which may result in higher maintenance costs and other problems.

## SENIOR COMMUNITIES

Communities catering to active seniors have become very popular and the Association is an essential element to provide recreational and maintenance services to an aging population. In addition to offering a more social environment, security and health related services; retired individuals have more free time and often enjoy the opportunity to be involved in their communities and special interest clubs. There may be an adjustment for seniors who have lived in single family homes without common area rules. Single or widowed individuals may benefit from the support, companionships, services and clubs common in Senior Communities. There are usually more volunteers available to assist the Association, but meetings can become more contentious as dissident individuals or groups may be more active as retirees have more free time to question HOA operations.

## PRESTIGE/LUXURY HOAS

Some of the country's premium or prestige properties are in HOAs because they desire high security and strict architectural regulations. Buyers should be aware of the financial responsibilities that may go along with being in such an HOA. In addition to high monthly fees, luxury HOAs may have major unexpected special assessments voted by the membership for special projects or programs without a great concern for the ultimate cost.

## DOUBLE TAXATION

Many Cities/Counties are requiring developers to provide HOA maintained streets, landscaping, parks, etc. in order to obtain new subdivision approval because local governments do not want the financial responsibility. HOA members often pay the same property taxes as the other city residents but do not receive the same city services. Legal challenges to this situation have not generally been successful, but political pressure may be more effective since the Association members can become a voting block.

## IS BUYING IN AN HOA BEST FOR YOU

As to the basic question, if being in an HOA is better, it depends. A non-HOA property is probably a better investment if the property and neighborhood are well maintained. In an HOA, there may be special life style amenities as well as a funded, monitored and scheduled minimum maintenance standard for all properties. In non-HOA neighborhoods this will not be the case and deteriorated or run down adjacent properties may affect the quality of living and/ or diminish area property values. Also a consideration for being in an HOA may be related to a realization that as people age they may not be able to adequately maintain property or in situations where a spouse is left alone, an HOA could provide desired and needed services and security.

## INDIVIDUALISTS

Some people should not live in an HOA if they have strong feelings about their individual rights. An owner will not have the choice of what color the house or front door is painted or items that may be placed in the front yard. Additions or modifications are usually controlled by strict architectural review procedures. If you like to work on your car in the front yard or store material in visible areas, an HOA is not for you.

***** 

## HOA HOUSING TYPES

Homeowner Associations serve a variety of housing types such as Cooperatives, Condominiums and Master Plan Communities. These developments are generally referred to as Common Interest Developments (CIDs).

In a COOPERATIVE, the HOA is the holder of title to the entire development, with the residents being stock holders with the right to occupy a specific apartment. Also known as Co-ops, in this type of development the Board of Directors have greater authority over who may buy and what type of improvements may be made. Financial income and asset minimums may be set by the Board of Directors and buyers required to submit verifiable financial information. Obtaining financing will be more difficult and selling may also be affected.

In a CONDOMINIUM, the property owner has title and exclusive use of their unit, which may be an individual parcel or air space, with joint ownership of the common area that is the responsibility of the HOA. Condominium HOA responsibilities may be simple such as roofs or exterior painting or in very complex structures, such as in high rise buildings, include all plumbing, electrical, elevators, etc., affecting every resident being serviced by the Association. TOWNHOUSES are a type of Condominium that does not have a unit below or above, and title may include the land directly under the unit.

A PLANNED DEVELOPMENT (PUD), sometimes referred to as a Master Planned Community or a Planned Unit Development, generally has individual titles to each parcel, with joint ownership of the common area. Individual properties may be freestanding homes or have common walls. They may appear to be regular subdivisions but may have private streets, clubhouses, pools or other recreational facilities as common area. Controlled access and special landscaping are also common amenities of Planned Developments. PUDs may include a variety of housing types; single family homes, townhouses, multi-story structures and even commercial areas. These multi-use developments will usually have a master association, with sub-associations for the different types of homes, uses or buildings.

## WHY HOAS WERE CREATED

A developer decides that the best way to sell homes is to create a community with special facilities, open space, landscaped areas or perhaps controlled access. New buyers agree that having property and amenities shared by all owners with someone to enforce neighborhood standards is a good idea. Who would manage these common facilities? The City or County would not take on such responsibility because the land is privately owned and not generally open to the public. The Developer will eventually sell all lots and go on to other projects and thus does not want the continuing responsibility. That left the residents. Since they owned the shared property, they should have the responsibility for its maintenance. The developer creates a written contract between the new property owners and Homeowner Association indicating the authority and responsibilities of the parties and how it will be funded.

## *WHO AND WHEN?*

Like a person or a government, the Homeowners Association has a life history of its own: a birth, infancy, adolescence and maturity. The developer conceives and designs the Association and gave birth to it in legal documents recorded with the subdivision, commonly called "Declaration of Limitations, Covenants, Conditions & Restrictions", and appoints an initial Board of Directors, usually developer employees. During the infancy period of construction and sales, the Association is dependent on the developer for finances and leadership. As the community matures and homes sold, the Association becomes more independent of the developer's support and control and changes to a governance by the homeowners themselves.

The original governing documents are often complex, legal, recorded instruments by the Developer in order to maintain control and have the ability to add to or change things to reflect market and sales conditions until all units are sold. The Developer often emphasizes to the initial buyers that the documents will keep the assessments low and preserve the community as it was built. Unfortunately as the community ages and market conditions change after the Developer is gone, there may be a need or desire to make changes and costs usually increase as facilities age. This lack of flexibility to some owners may be considered a benefit, while at other times it may be detrimental to the community.

## *WHAT DOES THE ASSOCIATION DO?*

The primary purpose of an Association is to protect livability, common areas and enhance the value of the property owned by the members. This is done by providing for the physical maintenance and operation of the common areas and in some cases actual maintenance of the exterior of each residence. The Association is also responsible for enforcing the rules, architectural controls, complying with governmental regulations, and having an effective communications with members. Members have the opportunity to determine how the Association operates through participation at meetings and serving on the governing body.

There are some things the Association does not do. It is not a political organization to influence outside issues and elections. On rare occasions, the Association may become active on a local single civic issue if it affects the property values of all members. The Association is not a forum for individual disputes between neighbors or civil legal matters. The Association does not have police powers, but operates within the recorded documents, which in essence are a contract between the owners and the Association.

## *HOW THE ASSOCIATION FUNCTIONS*

Homeowner Associations are administered by a Board of Directors, elected by the property owners, usually one vote per parcel, but votes may also be allocated on some other basis, such as size of the unit. A typical Board has five members, but may be three for small Association, or for larger developments, seven, nine or any number. My experience is that the larger the Board the more time consuming it is to make decisions. It is best that terms be staggered so that the entire Board does not change at once. In order to run for the Board normally a candidate must be a property owner in good standing. Association officers are usually elected by the Board from its members. The Board may be assisted in its duties by voluntary committees of Association members as listed in the CC&Rs or designated by the Board.

Each homeowner is involved in the Association in some manner. Involvement may only mean paying your monthly assessment on time, cooperating with the Association and participating where you will be most effective, even if that means you only vote at the annual meeting. You may wish to take a more active role, serve on the Board of Directors or on a committee. If you do become actively involved, you will find it a rewarding, educational experience, and both you and the Association will benefit, provided the time and effort is taken to understand and comply with your documents and applicable laws.

## OPERATING RULES

Association By-Laws establish the rules for conducting Board elections and meetings. It also outlines procedures for recalling members of the Board of Directors. There are two types of meetings conducted by an Association, the GENERAL MEMBERSHIP ANNUAL MEETING and BOARD OF DIRECTORS meetings.

The ANNUAL MEMBERSHIP MEETING of all property owners usually provides for the election of Board members or other actions that require approval of a majority of owners. All owners have the right to participate in the meetings by speaking, proposing motions and voting, with the HOA required to provide advanced meeting notice. The challenge for an effective general membership meeting is obtaining a quorum. Most elections or other actions require a majority of the members be present or represented by proxy. Some actions may require a two thirds affirmative vote. Apathy can be a major problem with non participation members in reality being a "NO" vote since many actions requires a specific number of affirmative votes. For elections, where there is no quorum for the first meeting, the attending members may adjourn the meeting to a later date, usually one to four weeks later, and then the quorum requirement may be reduced. The quorum issue is usually covered in the By Laws, or in the State Corporations Codes, if the Association is incorporated.

Attracting dedicated and informed members to serve on the Board of Directors may be difficult due to the time involved and the complexity of the Association's operations. Board of Director members have fiduciary responsibilities and are often subject to verbal abuse from owners who object to rules enforcement, assessment increases or other difficult issues that must be dealt with. In small Associations the Board may actually be doing much of the work that is performed by employees or contract professional personnel in larger Associations. It is particularly difficult for members to personally enforce rules, fines, vehicle towing against their neighbors and is best handled by an independent staff or contracted personnel.

Following the election of new Board members, the Board usually reorganizes itself by selecting a President, Vice President, Secretary and Treasurer. The Board may be assisted by volunteer committees, which can be sounding boards for the community to review and recommend policies and programs. Some committees, such as the Architectural Review Committee, may be established in the CC&Rs, while others may be created for a special study or activity. Some typical special committees can be: Landscape, Security, Social, Sports, Emergency Preparedness, Budget or Finance.

BOARDS OF DIRECTORS MEETINGS are for the purpose of conducting routine business of the Association. Although open to attendance of all members, Board meetings generally do not permit members participation unless invited. It is recommended that Boards have a "public comment" portion for their meetings to permit members to make a short presentation on items on the agenda or to request information, but should set a time limit and not engage in dialog. Boards may meet monthly or on schedules determined by the amount of items needing review or action.

Agendas and minutes of the Board meeting must be available to members on request. Board members have a fiduciary responsibility to the Association and must act in a manner that is in the best interests of the Association and excuse themselves if there is any personal conflict of interest. Board members should be familiar with their powers, duties and responsibilities under the law and their governing documents. Board members who exceed their authority or do not follow accepted business practices may face increased liability, including personal liability.

The Board and Committee members donate their time and energy and receive no remuneration. When making requests to these volunteer groups, it is generally best to put comments in writing so that concerns or suggestions are clearly thought out and also that they can be transmitted, where appropriate, to more than one group. Also, try to be positive rather than antagonistic since these people are your neighbors and are giving of their individual time to serve the entire community. Often those that complain the most, do little to assist or offer positive suggestions. Why not get involved, run for the Board or volunteer for a Committee?

## NOMINATING COMMITTEES

Having a Nominating Committee to solicit and encourage members to run for the Board can be an important factor in maintaining an active and qualified Board of Directors. The Committee should not limit any member from being a candidate and it is a policy decision as to if the Committee recommends an actual slate of candidates. The primary purpose of the Committee should be to make the membership aware of the pending election, members' opportunity to serve on the Board, and the duties of a Board member. Often very qualified members are reluctant to nominate themselves but when asked or encouraged to do so, are more likely to become active.

Suggested membership on the Nominating Committee should be former Board members and Committee Chairpersons, who will be most aware of the requirements for serving on the Board.

## *ASSOCIATION IS A BUSINESS*

Although many owners deal with their Associations as though they were social or informal groups, they are BUSINESSES. Large Associations may have annual budget of thousands of even millions of dollars and large Reserves that need to be safely invested. The Association may encompass real estate valued in the millions of dollars with the responsibility to protect and enhance that value. Although a Non-profit Corporation, like any business, the Association must comply with governmental regulations, as well as follow the recorded CC&Rs. To be successful it must operate smoothly and efficiently, key elements being:

(1) Economical and satisfactory operation and maintenance of facilities and services;

(2) Compliance with the Association's documents, State and Federal Laws;

(3) Accurate and forward looking budgeting;

(4) Assessments that support cost of managing and operating the Association and its facilities as well as setting aside reserves for replacements and emergencies;

(5) Swift, judicious and impartial enforcement of regulations;

(6) Communication and participation with homeowners through the Association Board, committees and employees or contractors.

## *EMPLOYEES OR CONTRACT STAFF*

To implement the actions and policies of the Board of Directors and serve the needs of members, may require paid employees or out sourced services through independent contractors. A small Association may have volunteers coordinating independent contractors on an informal basis, which is generally referred to as Voluntary Self Management. Medium sized Associations often contract with a CID Management Company for shared services with other Associations to collect assessments, prepare bids, deal with contractors, and attend Board meetings. Large Associations may choose to hire a full time on-site manager and association employees for all services. In some cases, the Association may choose to use a combination of its own employees and continuing contractors. An example would be having an on-site manager and office employees who deal directly with residents, but contracting for other services such as financial, maintenance and security.

There are some services that are generally contracted on an as needed basis, such as tree trimming or street maintenance, because it is done on a seasonal basis and may require specialized equipment. Legal services may also be contracted on a part time or on-call basis. Attitude and image of local staff is very important when there is an on-site office or access control personnel. Employee turnover, be they direct or contract personnel, should be minimized because of the negative effect on continuity, cost and image. Turnover is an indication that salaries are not competitive or that staff recruitment and screening is not being properly handled.

Cost is probably the reason that most Associations contract with a management company rather than having their own employees. The proposals or contracts with a management company should be carefully reviewed because their base fee to the Association may be lower because they charge additional premium charges for service to residents, sale transfer fees, over time for late meetings, copies, etc.. A drawback to contracting is that the Association must generally adapt to the procedures of the contractor and the importance of your account may determine the quality of service received. Also finding a quality and dependable contractor has the same challenges as selecting quality full time employees.

There currently are no significant requirements for being an Association manager or operating a management company, although several professional organizations do have educational and certification programs. Unfortunately the public and boards of directors have not generally recognized or rewarded managers who work to achieve advanced education or experience. Most Boards of Directors also do not use professional recruitment screening for selecting employees or management companies. It would be appropriate to have an experienced manager screen applications and check references so that the Board is only considering qualified individuals and thus can concentrate on the finalists to determine who is best for their organization. References and bonding is particularly important when selecting a Management Company because of their access to the Association's funds.

A clear line of authority and responsibility for supervision of employees or contractors must be adopted by the Board of Directors. Employees and contractors must know who can give direct orders, change procedures and monitor costs. In a small Association, individual Board members may coordinate specific budgets or contracts, but direction must come from the Board as a whole. Where there is an on-site manager or contract management company, direction must come at the Board of Directors meetings to the manager who will deal with employee or contractors. It must also be made clear to individual homeowners that they can not give orders to employees or contractors. Requests for special services from homeowners to employees should be acknowledged and forwarded to management or the Board. Employees can indicate to owners that it would be better for them to contact the Association office directly since there may be questions from the manager or applicable information available that the employee does not have. A written service request process is desirable to provide for follow up and a time line record.

A common question to an on-site manager is, "What does the Association do for my monthly assessment?" This question usually comes after an owner has asked for some special service which may not be covered under the CC&Rs, or if covered is taking too long to accomplish, in the member's opinion. Most of the services that an Association provides are taken for granted, such as maintaining landscaping and entries, operating pools or clubhouses, maintaining streets, enforcing the CC&Rs and reacting to homeowners requests for services and information. Owners should be regularly informed through newsletters, Board meeting minutes or other means of work that is underway or pending.

As our society becomes more complex, a lot of energy and expense is taken up by compliance with governmental regulations, insurance protection and litigation. The Association's efforts and activities for the preservation and enhancement of CID property values and to provide an environment for the safe enjoyment of its residents often takes more time than can meet residents' expectations, which are often unrealistic. With the growing problems of litigation the HOA Board or employees may need to react to situations in a more conservative manner to protect the Association from liability or legal entanglements, which may be causing unexpected delays or inaction.

# WHO DECIDES HOW AN HOA OPERATES

The members of the Association direct the operations of the Association through their elected Board of Directors. Monthly or on some other announced schedule, the Board regularly schedules meetings to conduct business. REGULAR MEETINGS of the Board of Directors are to conduct the routine business of the Association and may be attended by property owners. Occasionally the Board may adjourn to an EXECUTIVE SESSION to conduct owner hearings, consider contracts or deal with pending litigation. Executive Sessions are not open to the public due to confidential or privacy issues which are generally defined by law.

Members may request items be placed on the Board's agenda by sending in a written request. Requests for Board consideration should be specific and include appropriate back up information. An agenda with backup material is usually delivered to Board members a few days prior to the meeting so they can review the issues and perhaps request additional information. As previously indicated, all meetings of the Board, except Executive sessions, are open to members to observe, however the purpose of the meetings is to conduct the business of the Association and only Board members may vote on issues. Minutes of the Board's meeting and actions should be posted and available to members in a timely manner.

Dealing with difficult people can be a challenge at Board meetings because owners may feel they are entitled to special consideration and there may be personal relationships as neighbors. Establishing and adhering to meeting rules, with the chairperson maintaining control by requiring recognition to speak, staying on the agenda, and following parliamentary rules are critical. When there are a large number of attendees or individuals who regularly appear on the same subject, it is appropriate for the chairperson to explain the meeting rules, time limits and in some cases the Board may request that written slips be submitted indicating the speaker's name, address and subject so that they may be taken in an order and not be repetitious. Dialog between the resident and Board members should be avoided with requests for information handled by an indication that questions will be answered in writing or set as a future agenda item.

## DETERMINING WHERE THE MONEY IS SPENT

The annual budget of the Association estimates the projected levels of expenditures for the fiscal year, which may begin on January 1 or have a fiscal year with a different starting date. This annual budget not only sets the level of services and improvements, but determines the monthly assessment that each property will be required to pay for the next twelve months. The approval and monitoring of the budget together with the selection of employees or contractors who deliver necessary services, is the most important function of the Board of Directors.

Although the budget preparation schedule will vary due to the size of the Association, generally, about midway through the fiscal year, committees and residents make recommendations on the desired level of service or special projects to be considered in the next fiscal year. Staff working with the Board or sometimes a Budget Committee develops estimates and recommendations for the new fiscal year and prepares a preliminary budget. The Board of Directors evaluates and modifies the preliminary budget and should provide hearing opportunities for property owners to comment and when appropriate, the budget is adopted.

Some CC&Rs or State Laws require that copies of the adopted budget and notice of the new assessment amount be mailed to all owners prior to the beginning of the new fiscal year. Although many items are discretionary levels of services, there are items that the Board must include to meet legal or fiduciary obligations and maintain assets, including such items as insurance and adequate reserves. The Association budget, although larger, is much like any resident's budget who has a fixed income and must project costs a year in advance. The Association like every property owner continually faces inflationary increases such as utilities, insurance, labor costs, supplies and government mandated costs.

## SUCCESSFUL BIDDING

A major factor in the budget process is obtaining competitive bids, which involves a lot more than just the specifications. The Association desires to get the best work at a reasonable price and the vendor desires to do quality work that will provide a profit. There should be as much concern when a bid comes in too low as when it is too high. If the bidder has overlooked a costly item and then gets the contract at a price that will not be profitable, the association will not get a quality job or the contractor could go bankrupt.

There is always pressure from some owners to obtain the lowest price, but when the work is being done these same owners will expect quality work and if there are unexpected problems they will expect the contractor to absorb the costs. Often the Association's estimates are based on old cost figures or unit costs that may not reflect unique problems or inflation. Also the Association may be more concerned with inconvenience to members, where the contractor will be more interested in getting the job done as fast as possible. A solution to dealing with this difference in priorities is to meet with the contractors prior to the bidding and discuss the Association's expectations so that they may be reflected in the bid. Bidders may be met individually or as a group.

The complexity of bid specifications and contracts is also a growing challenge. Complex bids can take a lot of time and be costly to several bidders when obviously only one will be successful. If a contractor must bid five or six jobs to get one, that cost will be added to their overhead. Going out to bid to often on continuing service contracts can also have a negative long range affect. If a landscaper or other service provider bids a project two or three times and never gets the contract, they will eventually stop bidding and the Association will get a negative reputation in the industry. This also applies to changing service providers every year to save a few dollars. Eventually it will be more costly as contractors cease to bid or the quality of service drops.

Let vendors demonstrate ways to save money on the bids by permitting alternate bids. Require the bidder to meet specifications as written for competitive purposes, but permit addendum alternate bids that may substitute a cheaper product or utilize a different construction technique or equipment. The alternate bid can then be evaluated after the bidder is chosen.

On continuing service contracts, vendors should be treated similar to Association staff. Have regular contact with vendors and don't treat them as an enemy that is attacked or belittled at public meetings. If there are problems with the service, work to correct the problem rather than placing blame. There are times when contractors will be changed due to cost or the desire to try a new provider. Don't burn your bridges, the new contractor may not work out and you may want to bring back the previous vendor.

How vendors are treated will influence their desire to keep you as a customer and the Association's reputation as a good place to do business. Pay bills on time and do not hold up a $5,000 payment if there is a dispute over a $500 item. It is appropriate to hold back the five hundred dollars, but not the entire payment.

The Association should strive to build long term relationships with contractors or vendors rather than thinking of each as a one time event. This becomes very important in emergency situations when weather, earthquakes or other natural disasters may stress vendors' ability to meet demands. Which association is going to get immediate attention? Not the association that goes out to bid each year, regularly changes vendors and is only interested in the lowest price. In the long run the lowest price may end up being the most costly.

Make reputation and references an important part of the bid process. No matter how complete the specifications and contracts may be, nothing is as good as the integrity and experience of the vendor. Unfortunately we have gotten away from the days when an individual's hand shake meant a lot, but complex contract and litigation is not a desirable way to do business.

## ASSESSMENT DETERMINATION

After the budget is adopted, miscellaneous income from fees, interest, etc., is deducted and the remaining budget projection is divided by number of properties to determine the annual assessment and then this amount is divided by 12 to set the monthly assessment. Routine maintenance, replacements and repairs are included in the budget as well as reserves and emergency contingencies. The Association is not unlike a personal budget, where one estimates as close as possible, but must always be prepared to handle unknown events. In addition, the CC&Rs or State Laws may set limitations on the amount of increases in regular assessments or the amount of special assessments that may be made by the Board, without approval of a majority of the owners.

**SPECIAL ASSESSMENTS** are usually unexpected costs that were not funded in an annual budget or as new projects and may require special notice to the membership. Special Assessments are often triggered by natural disasters, litigation or other uncontrolled events and should be a last resort, due to the hardships it may create on property owners with limited incomes.

Like any business, the Association may be faced with unanticipated inflation, emergency situations or other unexpected happenings and sometimes has trouble collecting assessments. In order for the Association to pay its bills, each owner must pay monthly assessments in a timely manner or they can be subject to late fees that with continued non-payment are subject to lien and foreclosure of the delinquent owner's property. Residents who object to late fees must be reminded that the fee is not a profit to the Association but offsets added costs incurred in accounting, sending out late notices and processing lien notices. Also the Association may incur penalties for late payments on its financial obligations if payments are not made in a timely manner because there are not assessment funds available. A convenient way to avoid late payments is to utilize the automatic debit services, usually available at no extra cost.

In comparing assessment rates with similar associations, it is important to determine what services or unit utilities are actually covered. In many cases an Association with a higher monthly fee may be the better value because of items that are included, which otherwise would be charged to the individual property owner. Often an Association includes cable television, internet, earthquake insurance or even electricity in some high rise buildings. The Association may be able to get cheaper bulk rates and save on individual installation costs. Also are there additional fees for use of recreational facilities or is everything included in the monthly fee? Also a larger number of units in an Association can be a major factor resulting in lower overhead costs per unit.

## RESERVES

As major facilities age and the need for modernization or replacement becomes a reality, the importance of including a Reserve Fund in the budget should be a priority. The challenge for older developments is to make up for lost years when no funds were set aside in their budgets. Major buildings or their important components need to be assigned a life expectancy and then each year a proportionate amount of money should be set aside to pay the estimated cost when the replacement needs to be done. The Reserve fund should also build in a factor for interest generated and an inflation factor for increasing costs. The importance of Reserves may be influenced by the component, obviously the replacement of condominium roofs must be done when there are leaks, where a problem with a swimming pool is not as critical because the pool may be temporarily closed. Caution must be taken that the Board does not use the Reserves as a slush fund for pet projects that were not budgeted. Some residents will object to a Reserve Fund but will wish to let future owners worry about paying for modernization or replacements. Reserve requirements may be addressed in the Association documents or in some State laws. Boards that do not budget for Reserves should consider having all owners vote on the subject to avoid potential claims that the Board did not meet it is fiduciary responsibility. There are Reserve Consultants who specialize in preparing Association Reserve Studies which Board members should review annually and annually inform residents of the Reserve process, criteria used in the study, and the funding level.

## TAXATION

Non Profit Mutual Benefit Corporations do file and pay income tax on certain types of incomes. There is a choice on alternate tax filing forms that should be evaluated by the Association CPA and the tax filing can be included with the annual audit bidding. A few Homeowner Associations have been able to obtain a full tax exempt status based on being a charitable public service organization, but the restrictions are very limiting and complex. The major benefit to the exempt status is the ability to receive tax deductible donations. State tax filing is also required for States that have income taxes.

## HOA STREETS/CONTROLLED ACCESS

Private streets are often a primary responsibility and cost for HOAs. Since police agencies will not patrol private streets, Association members, employees or contracted private security will be needed to enforce parking and traffic violations. Guests and service vehicles can be a problem since violation fines can not be collected from them because they are not owners covered under the documents. Owners who authorize entry may be charged for the violations of their guests, but this will be objected to by most owners. Preventive maintenance such as slurry and seal coating programs must be scheduled and budgeted to avoid costly street rebuilding. Traffic safety signing and markings with patrolling can also be a concern to avoid liability and to obtain adequate insurance at a reasonable cost.

Gating to provide controlled access has become a popular amenity, although the term "security" is not usually used due to law suits for implied special protection when there are property losses or criminal activities. Board of Directors should take care not to make statements that members could interpret as promises to the membership for their safety and security. Gating in some cases is an image or prestige factor. Manned gates are the most desirable but also can be very costly. The technology for unmanned gates in recent years has greatly improved where by transponders can be individually identified, monitored and deactivated when property is sold or transponders lost or stolen. Double gates and mechanical spikes can limit entry to one car per opening to prevent unauthorized follow through vehicles. It is strongly recommended that gates have surveillance cameras with 48 hour recorders to identify violating attempts or damage to vehicles who may claim equipment malfunctions. In my experience, Associations have avoided substantial claims and litigation costs when it is known that there were recordings of actual happenings. Video surveillance can also be used for pools, club houses and maintenance yards as a deterrent against theft and vandalism.

## NO ONE'S PERFECT

HOA directors, committees and employees are usually dedicated to maintaining their community as a safe, special place to live and play. Nothing is always perfect, so when something needs changing or improving, bring it to the attention of the HOA Board or manager in a calm and timely manner. Constructive criticisms are usually appropriate, but remember in an Association with many members, there will be conflicting views and most final decisions are compromises. Although there is a desire to satisfy member needs and wants, there are often CC&R or budget limitations on the ability to do certain things. Particularly where potential litigation is involved, the process can be time consuming. Timing is also critical, sometimes things can be done right away, at other times, and it may have to wait its turn or for future budgeting.

When requesting service or bringing an issue to the attention of the HOA, indicate if it is a real emergency, but don't exaggerate the situation as it only wastes time and resources. Requests should be in writing because it provides a paper trail and time frame for follow up. Also the extra effort required for requests or complaints in writing usually indicates the issue is not just a spur of the minute event or grandstanding.

If things are done right, it's nice to hear about that too. Board members and volunteers give a lot of time and energy, without expectation of reward, but a thank you from their neighbors is always appreciated.

## *LEGAL DOCUMENTS*
### MASTER REGULATIONS SET THE RULES

When a group of people share property or property rights (easements), rules must be set down for its use and how changes can be made. These rules and their enforcement are essential to preserve property values and protect the quality of living in the community. When the developer planned a project, a set of legal documents were developed which establishes an Association, governs its operations, and provided rules for the process for creating rules for use of properties in the community. The legal documents generally consist of the following:

ARTICLES OF INCORPORATION - Establishes the non-profit Association and its purpose, structure and powers.

DECLARATION OF RESTRICTIONS - Covenants, conditions, restrictions and reservations, commonly referred to as "CC&Rs", are also recorded against all lots within the Association. The CC&Rs detail each owner's property rights, as well as their obligations to the Association. Each property buyer should receive a copy of the CC&Rs through escrow or at the title recordation, and they are listed in the title policy conditions for each property. Unfortunately few owners take the time to read and evaluate these important controls and obligations on their property use.

CC&Rs cover a variety of subjects effecting property use and enjoyment, such as RV and boat storage, nuisances, commercial activity, fire control, signage, and all improvement activities. The CC&Rs can be amended at various times by a vote of the owners, which when approved will also be recorded against the property. It is difficult to change or amend the CC&Rs because it takes a fixed percentage affirmative vote and a non voter is counted as a "NO" vote. Thus apathy is the main challenge to overcome. Changes are generally not proposed unless they are widely supported, but getting everyone to vote is the main hurdle.

BY-LAWS - Establishes rules for how the Association operates, membership, voting rights, meeting notice and quorum requirements, election or removal of Board of Directors, powers and duties of the Board, officers and committees, and record keeping and assessment authority. The By-Laws are primarily concerned with the mechanics of running the Association and assigning responsibility for decision making for day to day operations.

## *INSURANCE POLICIES*

Protecting the Association and members' common area property is an important responsibility of the HOA. The Board will need to decide the level of insurance coverage as compared to the cost, which must be passed on in the assessment to owners. Insurance can be very complicated and use of an experienced specialist is strongly recommended. In addition to the amount, special hazard coverage, such as earthquake, tornado, flood, storm, etc, will need to be evaluated. Some of these decisions may need to be communicated to members and in some cases scheduled for a vote. Bonding of employees or contract management should also be a priority to protect against financial irregularities or losses.

Insurance is an important offset against legal costs although there can also be a concern that insurance companies will pay nuisance claims to avoid legal expenses. The handling of claims and their disposition should be monitored in order to avoid encouraging claims which ultimately increase future insurance premiums. Directors and Officers (D&O) insurance should be obtained to protect volunteer Board members from being sued as individuals by dissent groups. In addition to covering common area property and generally liability, do not overlook Workers Compensation Insurance even if there are no direct employees. Workers Compensation costs are based on payroll so will have a minor minimum charge for coverage in case of claims from individuals that may not be clearly independent contractors. Unfortunately, potential litigation continues to be a growing problem in our society that requires better record keeping, accident reporting, and use of video cameras to record any event that has the potential for a claim.

## ARCHITECTURAL CONTROL

Most Associations have an Architectural Committee (AC), composed of property owners who review all plans and may approve, deny or approve with conditions all exterior applications. Depending on the complexity of the project, samples or exterior drawings may be required. Some Associations notify neighbors about exterior changes, not because their approval is needed, but so that they have an opportunity to comment.

The AC often has a difficult job because most property owners resent limitations on what they want to do, and some neighbors don't want construction that will restrict their views or privacy or just object to change. Some of the regulations, such as set backs are very specific, while other areas such as design, mass or color, are more subjective. Often there may be conflicting interpretations of the CC&Rs and the Architectural Committee and Board must set standards, which may be subjective.

It is important to be familiar with architectural controls and work with the staff and committee when making any exterior change on your property, including fencing and landscaping. This will avoid unnecessary mis-understandings which inevitably cause delays and extra expense. With property disclosure laws now in effect, it could be a future problem in any sale or property transfer if Association or City building laws have not been followed. A serious problem is created when an owner get approval for a modified plan and then constructs the original unapproved plan, and that is why there should be a final inspection on all construction.

## ASSOCIATIONS WORKING TOGETHER

HOA members may participate in both the national Community Associations Institute (CAI) and in some State Associations where Homeowner Associations work to develop consistent policies, educate members and strive to influence supportive governmental legislation. In several States there are CID chapters to share information between Association Boards, managers and vendors. Although efforts continue to encourage Board member training and the development of professional standards for staff, most Associations to do not take the time to become involved. Association budgets have not generally funded the costs of training nor rewarded employees for attaining special certifications because most owners do not appreciate the fact that Associations are complex businesses with major assets. There are few requirements for managing an Association and there have been unfortunate cases of embezzlement of HOA funds.

# LITIGATION

A growing challenge to all Associations is litigation which is an expensive and a slow process for resolving CC&R disputes. On occasion legal action is the only recourse when there are flagrant violations or non compliance after reasonable notices are ignored. The Association is often criticized for it taking too long to enforce regulations, without a realistic appreciation for the time and expense when the courts must be used. Members should be reminded that when they sue the Association they are in essence suing themselves and their neighbors.

The criteria for selecting legal counsel to advise the Association can be very important and should emphasize resolving issues rather than winning at all costs. My experience has generally been that the only winners in lawsuits are both sides' attorneys. The use of Alternate Dispute Resolution is encouraged, which can involve a mediation or arbitration process as a step prior to litigation. There are great hopes for this less expensive and faster way of solving conflicts, but it requires both parties to agree to participate. Care should be taken to select a mediator who understands HOAs and their governing documents.

# STATE/FEDERAL REGULATIONS

Some State Legislatures, such as California, Florida and Nevada, have enacted substantial regulations effecting Homeowners Association, in addition to regulations contained in State Corporation Codes. Some of the government codes preempt the CC&Rs while others only apply where the Association documents are silent. State and Federal Laws have also been changing regarding age or other civil rights restrictions which can place added responsibilities on all Associations. Unfortunately sometimes the Legislature or Courts over react to a perceived problem and create added unnecessary costs or operational complexity for every HOA. Often the Legislators or Judges are not well informed on how HOAs operate and have a tendency to treat them similar to Municipalities, which they are not. The critical difference is that an HOA does not have police powers or governmental immunity. Some State regulations are also delaying the possible foreclosure for non payment of assessments, not recognizing that services must continue to be provided and non paying members must be subsidized by the paying members.

## *HOA GOAL*

The protection, preservation and enhancement of property values and peaceful enjoyment by their residents is the primary purpose for most Homeowner Associations. The elected Board of Directors operates the Association on behalf of the owners, but the community will only achieve maximum success with the support, participation and commitment of all owners.

## *SUPPORT ENFORCEMENT*

It is a member's right to insist on effective and fair enforcement of rules. It is also a member's responsibility to support Association personnel and the Board when they are enforcing the rules. If rules need changing, campaign for changes. If rules are appropriate, support their enforcement.

To often all the work is left to "the other guys". Also remember, sometimes the correction of a violation, particularly on private property, takes a long time and is legally tedious. Don't assume nothing is being done, check with the Association as to the status. Be constructive in your comments. You will generally receive faster and better service if you convey reasonable requests and expectations. The three "Ps" pets, parking and parties seem to be the universal enforcement challenges for most Associations. Also it seems that approximate 2% of owners generate 90% of the enforcement problems.

## COMMUNICATING

The best way to know what's happening in an HOA is to read all material sent to your billing address, such as, the annual budget and other Association mailings. Suggested changes to the rules or requests for community improvements are best presented in writing. Anonymous complaints are difficult to deal with because additional information may be needed and it would be impossible to respond as to what action was pending.

The Association should communicate on a regular basis through a newsletter, emails, a web page and other appropriate methods. Newsletters or websites should be for dispensing factual information and projecting a positive image. Custom internet programs can be used to permit viewing of account balances, paying fees, registering for events or requesting services.

Websites in the Association's name should be registered to protect against other individuals using the Association name for their own use. In many cases it will be a real estate agent who desires to handle sales in the development. Unfortunately if acquired by an individual or dissident group it can be used to undermine the Board or Association image. Advertising in a newsletter or as a sponsor for a web site is debatable. Advertisers can offset the cost of newsletters and websites and be of value in gated communities where it is difficult for businesses to promote their desire to serve the community.

## PRESS/MEDIA RELATIONS

Someone should be designated to represent the HOA as a spokesman to respond to questions from media reporters or to handle unexpected events such as fires, accidents or other newsworthy items. In the past newspaper reporters would make efforts to get background information or attempt to have a secondary source before publishing stories, but this is no longer always the case.

Television and internet news sites now often go public with whatever information they may have available, often incomplete or totally one sided. Unfortunately the media is generally not friendly to HOAs. They often appear to be more interested in sensationalism than accuracy. It may partially be due to a lack of understanding about HOAs, but often it is due to there not being sources for the facts. National media on several occasions has been guilty of pandering to disgruntled persons under the guise of protecting the individual from a big bad HOA. Interviews with TV reporters should be cautiously undertaken because they may film for several minutes, but only broadcast a sound bite out of context.

In smaller communities it may be possible to develop a contact with the local reporter or news managers and offer to provide information and perhaps human interest material about the Association or its residents.

## PROMOTING AFTER THE DEVELOPER LEAVES

One of the major goals of Homeowners Associations is the preservation and enhancement of property values. However, very few associations have any activities or budget funds for promotional purposes. On the negative side, many gated developments have restrictions on open houses and real estate signs that may put their properties at a disadvantage in competing with sales of homes in similar developments. The challenge becomes more difficult when older developments are competing for buyers against new well advertised developments. The initial developer generally does extensive advertising and creates quality promotional material on their homes and property amenities. After the developer has completed the project and all units are sold, the promotion of the project ceases except for possible advertising by Real Estate Brokers with listings in the area.

There are a variety of things that can be done to promote a mature development, starting with the recognition that promotion of the project should be a priority. Some obvious things that are the Association's responsibility are the entries and physical monuments identifying the development. They may need updating or upgrading. Even basic things like paint colors may be outdated.

Maintaining a good relationship and working with the Board of Realtors should also be a priority. This does not mean giving up your signing or access rules, but Realtors should understand the benefits of the rules in maintaining the quality and security of the community. Efforts should be made to work with real estate sales people to assure that access and signing policies are reasonable. It is suggested that at least once a year Realtors be invited to an orientation meeting to explain association rules and allow them to make suggestions for improvements that would facilitate home sales.

Homeowners Associations have been on the defensive responding to assaults from the press, dissident owners groups, the legislature, litigation and some just generally mean-spirited people. The press likes to portray our communities as self serving when in reality the Associations are providing and maintaining facilities that would otherwise not be available. Residents need to be reminded that

HOAs provide for architectural controls and maintenance often not adequately covered by local ordinances. These activities improve property values for the whole community. Budgeting of funds and working to promote the community is a good investment to enhance property values over the long term.

## *DOING YOUR PART*

The key to a successful Association is the support and enthusiasm of its members. And since you are the member that means you. Apathy is the plague of Homeowners Associations. If no one attends meetings or participates, nothing gets done or perhaps a non representative few run things to the displeasure or detriment of the whole. Remember to achieve consensus everyone must participate and be willing to show consideration for the views and rights of others through compromise. This also means taking the time to find out the facts and not jump to conclusions from half truths, statements or emails that are critical of everything happening in the community. Become involved in the Association, serve on the Board, on a committee, or show support. You can also help the Association by always doing three things:

1. Pay your Association assessments on time;
2. Cooperate with the Association, follow rules, help where you can;
3. Participate in a meaningful and constructive way.

## *OUT OF CONTROL BOARDS*

On rare occasions, a Board of Directors can loose its way and become dictatorial and out of touch with the owners. Often the reason is due to apathy of the membership and lack of participation, thus letting small self serving group's control. Another reason may be that the Board is simply not following the Association documents and governmental regulations. Inadequate budgeting to keep assessments low and not adequately funding community maintenance can be another serious problem.

The solution is for members to get involved, attend and speak at meetings and put the Board members on notice of their fiduciary responsibilities. Written notice that the Board could also be held personally liable for their Board actions, or lack of action, may also get their attention. On a continuing basis encourage and support qualified candidates to run for the Board.

## SUMMARY/CONCLUSION

The decision to purchase a property in a Common Interest Development with a Homeowners Association will probably be ultimately determined by the desire to participate in the life style offered in the development. Prospective buyers should visit the property at various times to be sure that the activities and maintenance of the common areas meet expectations. It is also worthwhile to talk to existing residents and observe if the community has the age range and activities with which you will be comfortable.

Be sure to thoroughly read the CC&Rs and posted rules. Obtain copies of the Budget, Board minutes and community newsletters. Review the monthly financial reports, check the availability of reserve funds and ask if there is any pending litigation that could have a significant financial impact. Local Realtors can also be a good source of information on the history of an HOA.

For someone who has never lived in a Homeowners Association there could also be an adjustment to living in a more structured development. This is not all negative because it may be a pleasant surprise to have a home to enjoy without having to take care of maintenance while having community facilities available for recreational enjoyment.

There is little question as to the continuing importance of Homeowner Associations as a growing percentage of new developments are CIDs. The motivation is a combination of a desire by homeowners for amenities, higher density due to choice locations increased land costs, and local government's reluctance to take on the financial obligation of new subdivisions' public improvements. The value of your home, the quality of your community and the resulting pleasant life style depend on your Community Association. The success of your Association ultimately depends on your participation.

\*\*\*\*\*\*\*

# Part 2

## *RESPONSE TO QUESTIONS*

Following are previously published responses to questions received from residents or Board of Directors members concerning living and participating in Common Interest Developments. Opinions expressed are generalized and not intended to be a substitution for consulting with appropriate legal counsel or other professional advisors. Also a Homeowner Association's specific documents or unique State statutes could have resulted in a different answer to any specific situation.

### SHORTER BOARD MEETINGS

QUESTION: *How can Board meetings be kept shorter yet still be more productive? Do owners have the right to participate at all meeting?*
Boards and members must remember that the meetings are for the purpose of conducting the business of the corporation that manages the association and are not member forums. There are two types of Board meetings, the General Business Session, which is open to all members, and the Executive Session, which is not open to the members but is restricted to dealing with such items as litigation, personnel matters, contract negotiations and violation hearings. Although the General Session is open to attendance by any member, it does not mean members can participate in the Board discussions or deliberations.

It is a common practice and recommended that at the opening of the Board meeting there be a "Public Forum" at which members may comment on any subject including items on the agenda. Usually the Board adopts procedural rules such as a time limit (3 minutes) and speaker cards may be used to indicate the speakers name and subject. Members should be encouraged to submit their requests in writing and the Board should not generally enter into a dialog with speakers but indicate the subject will be reviewed and responded to later. Once the meeting is underway discussion should be limited to the members of the Board unless a member with special expertise is invited by the Chairman to provide answers to Board questions. If the Board is consistent in following this procedure, members will understand and make their comments at the Public Forum or submit written material.

Regarding the meeting, an agenda with written backup or exhibits should have been given to Board members in advance and an agenda posted for members to review. Except in emergency situations, matters should not be brought up that are not on the agenda. The chairman must follow the agenda and get closure before moving on to the next subject. Board members should have reviewed the agenda material and if there are questions regarding the backup, staff should be contacted before the meeting so the information can be available and presented to all the members at the meeting. An example of poor practices is the page by page review of the minutes at the meeting, which should have been read prior to the meeting and any corrections given in writing to the Chairperson.

A "Consent Calendar" is an excellent tool for handling routine items which may be listed with the recommended action and one motion made to adopt all items. If any Board member desires to discuss a consent calendar item, they may request it be removed from the list and discussed and acted on under new business. An agenda can include an estimated time allocation by each item as a method to limit discussion where there are a lot of items to be dealt with and a time limit for the meeting is desired. The Chairperson has the responsibility to keep the meeting moving and on subject, but needs the support and cooperation of all the Board members to do so. The members will also appreciate attending meetings that are short and productive.

## RULES ENFORCEMENT

QUESTION: *Why does it take so long for the association to get owners to comply with obvious rule violations?* **Most rules compliance is done through diplomacy, which often takes time. Associations do not have police powers and enforcement of the contractual agreements that established an association usually requires specific procedures to be followed. This has become even more complex by some additional States' legislation that requires additional time consuming processes. When violations are brought to most people's attention, they will comply within a reasonable time period. Sometimes there are extenuating circumstances that must be investigated and in some instances a resident will feel the rule is unreasonable or it doesn't apply to them.**

There are some people who should not have chosen to live in an association with rules and will require litigation measures to obtain compliance. The litigation process is both costly and time consuming and should only be used as a last resort. Because you don't see anything happening, don't assume nothing is being done, call your manager or Board member to explain the process.

## ANONYMOUS COMPLAINTS

QUESTION: *Why should I be requested to give my name when turning in a violation of association rules?*
Often anonymous requests for enforcement of rules are received where there can not be follow up or response because the information is incomplete. A contact person is often needed to verify information

or clarify what action can be taken. Most associations should have a policy of not disclosing the name of complainants unless it is necessary due to court action. Every effort should be made to avoid neighborhood feuds, which is a primary reason for not indicating the source of the complaint.

However, often the Board or staff is accused by the violator of harassing or discriminating against them and thus a third party complainant is desired. People don't like to get involved, but in many cases it is only by furnishing detailed observations that there can be sufficient information to take action. Often members do not communicate with a neighbor but needlessly involve the association rather than dealing with a problem directly. Issues such as how cars are parked or where pets are off the required leash could easily be politely mentioned to the offender who generally is more interested in complying with a neighbor's request than a letter or call from the association.

If you want to keep your community a good place to live, residents need to be involved and support association rules enforcement. If the rules are not appropriate or not enforceable, then they should be changed.

## SUPPORTING ENFORCEMENT

QUESTION: *How can the association get owners to support rules enforcement?*

There are several issues that influence a successful rules enforcement program that facilitates community support. First, rules must be reasonable and be communicated to members so their expectations are realistic. Don't over react by adopting a rule that negatively impacts the whole association for every situation. Rules enforcement must be equitable, consistent and disciplinary action must provide owners' due process rights.

All rules can not be enforced all the time, so rules may be selectively assigned priorities and residents encouraged to provide information as to when and where there are problems needing attention. Complainant's names should not be disclosed to violators to avoid facilitating neighborhood feuds. The number and type of violations should be communicated to owners in monthly newsletters so members are aware of what rule enforcement is taking place.

Technology may be one of our pitfalls in striving to build a sense of community, where the priorities have become efficiency rather than effectiveness. In order to reduce cost, staff has been reduced through automated phones, form letters and emails which have replaced personal contact. I support enforcement where personnel actually meet owners at their property and if they are not home, leave a door hanger with a phone number (sometimes cell) that a real person answers. It is also desirable to use warning notices with courtesy letters prior to actually giving citations and scheduling penalty hearings. Treat all owners as you would want to be treated and that violations may just be oversights.

It is true that some people should not live in an association, but once they are there, a priority should be to educate to inform what the rules are and why they are being enforced. Surveys show that the vast majority of residents are happy living in their HOA's, yet the media and the small percentage of disgruntled residents continue to project a negative untrue image. An additional challenge that faces older associations is the modernizing of their rules to meet changing times.

## BOARD AGENDAS
QUESTION: *Who should be the final authority on determining what goes on the Board agenda?*

The content of the Board agenda has become more important as some States are micromanage homeowner associations by requiring that agendas be posted to members in advance or there be no discussion or action on items not on the agenda, with minor exceptions such as emergency subjects. Usually the Board President is the final authority for the Board agenda however any Board member may request items is placed on the agenda. One should first check the Association's Bylaws and the appropriate Parliamentary Rules of Order, which should be listed in the Bylaws or adopted as a Board policy. Although any Board member may request an item be placed on the agenda, if the item is rejected by Board action, the member can not continually request it be placed on the agenda. Generally only a Board member that voted against acting on the item may request reconsideration. This restriction is to prevent an individual with a minority view point from continually rehashing the same subject.

Regarding homeowners requesting items be placed on the agenda, it is wise to require that items be in writing, including appropriate background information, and be presented sufficiently in advance to permit time to research the issue. Usually a week prior to the posting of the agenda is appropriate.

Many associations have a "public forum" prior to the Board business meeting to permit members to comment on any items on the agenda or subjects in need of Board consideration. Any subjects not on the meeting's agenda should not be discussed, but may be referred to staff or placed on a future agenda.

There are a variety of agenda formats, some simple one-liners, while large associations with full time staff may provide lengthy agendas with backup information. Efforts should be made to provide members attending the meeting with a summary agenda so they can understand the business before the Board. Board members should have received an advanced packet with more extensive detail and backup information. The chairperson may need to remind members attending the meeting of the difference between the annual meeting of members, where everyone may participate and the Board meeting which is for the purpose of conducting association business by the Board members. A well run, short productive business meeting will reflect a positive image for the association and foster quality candidates to serve on the Board.

## MEETING MINUTES

QUESTION: *What should be included in the minutes of the Board meetings? Should comments or quotes be included in the minutes?* Although a Board may establish a different policy on what may be included in its meeting minutes, the purpose of the minutes is to be a RECORD OF ACTION taken. Minutes should not attempt to be a transcript of statements made at the meeting. The minutes are an important historical record approving expenditures, policies and may be used as evidence in legal challenges and thus comments or discussions should not cloud or confuse the actions taken.

Minutes should include the time and place of the meeting, the type of meeting (regular, special, executive session), who was in attendance, a general description of matters discussed, any actions taken with the vote on all motions, the time of the next meeting, and the time the meeting was adjourned. Anyone invited to attend should be identified. The purpose of the Board meeting is to conduct the business of the Association and it needs to be made clear that members may attend and observe, but not participate unless invited.

It is recommended that a public forum be held at the start of Board meetings to give an opportunity for members to address the Board and bring matters to their attention. General subjects can be indicated as brought up at the open forum, but generally should not be dealt with unless already an agenda item. The annual meeting of the Association should not be confused with the Board meeting, in that the annual general membership meeting is for and by the members, with the Board's only role being to facilitate the meeting and provide information or an annual report of the association's activities.

Minutes or a summary of Board meetings should be available to members in a timely manner, except for Executive Sessions, which is not public information. However Executive Sessions need to be noted in the minutes of the next regular meeting. Because many Boards only meet monthly or quarterly, minutes marked as "Draft" may be posted or available to members until the final minutes are approved.

It is important in keep members informed of what actions are being taken by the Board, but use of a newsletter or other public information methods should be used rather than attempting to make the minutes a PR or forum publication. Keep the minutes as a basic record of actions taken.

## MEMBER SUPPORT OF CC&RS
QUESTION: *Any suggestions on how complaints about CC&R violations can be handled to obtain compliance and still improve member support?*
Teddy Roosevelt said it best, "walk softly but carry a big stick". Often violations are inadvertent and a polite reminder will solve the problem. A personal call, door hanger note or a courteous letter may be enough. If no compliance, a timely enforcement process should be started with a hearing before the Board and an appropriate penalty, which may be waived when there is compliance.

A basic step in any rules enforcement is educating all members on the CC&Rs and the current adopted rules. This is a continuing process because there are always new members moving in and long time residents' needing reminders. A regular newsletter including articles on the more common violations is a good communications tool. There needs to be an awareness of the Association's authority or often lack of authority regarding problems that can be deal with. Associations do not have police powers and may only deal with issues specifically addressed in the CC&Rs. Other enforcement agencies should be suggested where appropriate, such as the police, animal control, health department, etc..

Some states have mandated enforcement guidelines that need to be followed. Any delays required by law are often a problem to those homeowners complaining who may think that the enforcement process takes too long or that staff is not doing their jobs. Persons filing complains should be encouraged or even required to have their complaints in writing so they can be informed on follow up on what is taking place and also as a protection for the association who may be accused of being discriminatory or arbitrary. The name of the complainant should not be disclosed except if the matter ends up in litigation, where the information may be desired by the court. Rules are of no value unless enforced fairly and in a timely manner.

## CHANGING CC&RS

QUESTION: *Our CC&Rs are out dated and need amending but the Board appears to have given up because of the apathy of members to support change – any suggestions?*

Many associations are facing the challenge of getting members to support and vote for needed modernization of documents. Overcoming apathy and the status quo takes a lot of effort, good communications with members and broad based support. In many associations there can be a disconnect between the information the Board has and the information being communicated to the members. It is hard to get members to take the time to be informed on complex or long term issues, but the Board must strive to make the information available on a continuing basis.

My first suggestion would be to appoint a broad based CC&R Revision Blue Ribbon Committee to study and be the advocate for changes, conduct town hall meetings and circulate material to explain the proposed changes. This Blue Ribbon Committee should represent a cross section of the community, present and former Board members, and committee or club representatives. The current Board should not dominate the committee and disruptive owners should not be permitted to appoint themselves to the committee. A strong, fair and diplomatic chairperson should be selected to lead the committee.

The next suggestion is to make the changes as clear and simple as possible, not a lengthy legalistic document. It is not necessary to correct or solve all the association's problems at one time. It is good to build the changes around a popular issue that will motivate members to vote.

As we are all aware from Board elections, we rarely can get a quorum, so getting the necessary two thirds positive vote is the biggest problem in changing the CC&Rs. Non voters in essence are voting no, so the challenge is to get everyone to vote. Normally the election cut off date for ballots to be received is set, and as ballots are received they should be matched to membership rolls so you know the percentage received and who has not voted. The committee needs to continually contact those that have not voted and request they do so. I have had instances where the election date has been extended several times to get the necessary participation. Sometimes this requires some badgering and personal contact, such as delivering lost ballots. In one election for new CC&Rs, it failed because members objected to having to vote on all of the changes as a single issue rather than being able to vote on separate sections. It was a difficult decision to permit voting on separate sections because many sections were interdependent. However, when members were able to vote by sections, all the changes were approved. The opposition apparently was to the procedure rather than the substance.

There are usually members who question any change and think of situations or questions that can not be readily addressed. Try to maintain a positive and calm attitude and indicate their concerns will be taken into consideration. Arguing will accomplishing nothing. If the election results in majority support but lacks the two thirds requirement there may be the opportunity to go to court, which under certain conditions can let a majority vote approve the changes. Obviously legal counsel must be consulted on such issues. Modernizing your CC&Rs is worth the effort.

## COMMON AREA ENCROACHMENTS

QUESTION: *Although our CC&Rs indicate the Board may authorize expanding our patio into the common area, the Board indicates it will require approval of all owners – is there any alternative?*

This is a subject that should be reviewed with legal council prior to consideration of any transfer of exclusive use of common areas. In California, the State Legislature preempted an association's recorded documents or previously existing policies by requiring membership approval for granting of exclusive use common areas, with a few exceptions. This restriction applies to all association common areas, whether held in fee title or by easement. California requires that prior to the granting of any exclusive use of common area by the Board of Directors, it must be approved by at least sixty seven percent of the members, unless your CC&Rs specify a different percentage, although there are a few exceptions.

The protection and enhancement of the common area is a fiduciary responsibility of the Board of Directors. The granting of exclusive use could be an issue resulting in litigation and should be approached with great caution and a written legal opinion. Any action of the Board granting use or title to common area should be very public, with ample advanced notice to permit member comment prior to any final action.

## FINE CRITERIA
QUESTION: *What is the best method or criteria for a Board to determine the amount of fines or penalties for violations of association rules?*

There is no simple formula or rule for determining the amount of a fine or penalty for the violation of the governing documents or for the abuse or misuse of common area facilities. Although each case may be different, Boards must not be arbitrary or capricious. Some State Codes may require that a schedule of any monetary penalties must be adopted and distributed to each member, which is a good procedure even if not required. The most important fact to be considered is the purpose of the fine or penalty, which should be to obtain compliance, not to punish.

Just as each violation may be different, associations also may differ widely on the financial impact on a member's ability to pay and reaction to being fined. Obviously the members of an association of million dollar homes compared to a retirement community where members are living on social security may not have the same fine schedule. Many years ago I attended a meeting where they had a $10.00 fine for interrupting a speaker. When a well-to-do member was fined $10 for interrupting the speaker, he promptly gave the chairman a $100 bill, indicating that he would be interrupting the speaker several more times. Obviously this was not an effective way to obtain compliance.

Another factor is the ability of the association to collect fines. Some State Legislatures make it more difficult or in some cases more trouble than it is worth to collect monetary penalties. If they are never collected they will never be taken seriously. There are other penalties that may be considered, such as limiting use of recreation facilities, but this may have practical enforcement limitations. Another problem will be violations by guests or other visitors that are not easy to identify or enforce.

As you have doubtlessly noticed I have not specifically answered the question on how to determine the amount for fines or penalties, but rather indicated the factors that must be considered. Check with similar sized and home valued communities as to their fine scheduled and how effective their schedule has been in obtaining compliance.

## HANDLING RUMORS
QUESTION: *What can be done to stop rumors and counter negative attacks against the HOA Board or staff being circulated on the internet?*
The internet has become the fast, simple and inexpensive way to communicate, individually or with large groups. Unfortunately anyone can use web pages and mass email lists to spread rumors, half truths and negative remarks. The best counter action is to keep factual information flowing to Association members by use of your

own web page, email lists, regular newsletters and informative inserts in monthly billings.

If the rumors or negative information is being circulated by individuals who are just uninformed, make a personal contact and provide the right information. Be honest, factual and available. In cases, where you find the individual or group continue to circulate rumors after they have the truth, then you may need to write them off rather than wasting time and energy to give them accurate information. There are individuals who choose to be character and morale assassins and that may be a fact that must be lived with. The truth will come through if the factual information is continually provided. Acquire your Association web page name in .org, .com, and .net if they are still available. Most often the .com version of your Association name has been acquired by a Real Estate Broker as a marketing tool. Often dissident groups will attempt to set up a web page that looks like the official HOA web site.

If your Association does not have the skill to create a professional web site, there are several service providers that specialize in HOA sites. If the Board does not want to fund a professional service, consider having a commercial sponsor which may only involve having a link at the bottom of the home page that ties to a Realtor or other business wishing to offer services to homeowners.

## CONTROLLING LEGAL EXPENSES
QUESTION: *What can the Board do to minimize increasing legal expenses?*
There are several elements influencing legal costs. Obviously a major one is to avoid activities that have a higher potential for generating litigation. This should include consulting with legal counsel before questionable actions or activities are undertaken. The second is to

encourage the Board to maintain an attitude based on working to settle disputes through mediation and arbitration, without going to court "as a matter of principal". I have previously written about violation enforcement's primary tool being diplomacy rather than litigation. Often the choice of legal council sets the trend when attorneys are selected because of their aggressive litigation experience as opposed to resolving disputes through negotiation and compromise.

Another consideration in escalating legal costs in a dispute is the misconception that the lawyer is to be treated differently from other vendors. Where other vendors are generally subject to a competitive bid process, the lawyers are usually given a blank check for every assignment. While legal costs are often difficult to predict, most experienced lawyers should have an idea of what a dispute is going to cost at various stages.

Following are some reasons legal costs get out of control. Most often legal costs are not budgeted properly from the beginning. The cost to start litigation may not be that great, but the long term potential costs are often not considered. Estimates and reevaluation points need to be defined so that once a case is started it does not "take on a life if its own". Require input on a regular basis as to where things are going and what it is going to cost. Another problem is often a lack of an early response to problems that could have been handled easily and cheaply. Like maintenance items, dealing with things at an early stage is usually much cheaper. An example is a Board's not having legal counsel review contracts before execution. Another failure can be not examining and exploring alternatives or not negotiating. Lastly is to select the right attorney for each assignment. Associations tend to hire one attorney to handle all manners. Every matter does not just involve homeowner association law, but major issues may involve insurance, contracts, construction or many other law specialties. Going to court should be a last resort because the only sure winners will be the attorneys.

## ELECTION PROCESS

QUESTION: *I have heard that our Board election process must change although we are following the CC&Rs and the owners aren't concerned?*

Some states, such as California, have adopted election and voting procedures that preempt association documents and requires elections to have secret ballots and independent election inspectors. Also some Corporation Codes may apply regarding election of Board members. Many associations use post cards or other methods combined with proxies for conducting elections, which might no longer be permitted and will increase the cost of conducting elections due to additional notices and mailings. An open and neutral process for handling elections and the counting of the votes is critical to avoid negative rumors and to maintain confidence in the Association's management. There may also be limitations of what the Boards may publish in the election materials or limits to candidates statements. Any association publications near election times should be limited and carefully reviewed by legal counsel or the association may be required to publish and distribute material from any owner that has a different opinion.

Most new laws from State Legislatures are generally anti-association and written to empower the individual member. There often are a small number of individuals in an association that like to create friction or have an axe to grind and may use technical violations of these new laws to sue the association. The Legislature also does not appear to recognize or care about the additional costs due to new regulations that may result in higher monthly fees to the homeowners.

# BOARD MEMBER QUALIFICATIONS

QUESTION: *Can an Association require qualifications for candidates to run for the Board of Directors?*

As in most association rules or authority questions, first check your Association documents, particularly the Association By Laws, State Law and the Corporations Code, if you're Association is incorporated. If the law mandates that qualifications should be adopted, it is obvious that the requirements must be reasonable, but there are no particular guidelines for what the legislature or eventually the courts may regard as reasonable. Some sample requirements include requiring prior service on an Association committee, volunteer participation at community activities, commitment to be available to attend regularly scheduled Board meetings or participation in related organizations such as CAI, CMA or IREM.

Most association documents require that a member be in good standing, which is generally interpreted as being current in paying assessments. A requirement of prior service on an association committee must include the ability by any owner to serve on a committee and that there be a reasonable number of committees with a variety of interests. Any requirements must be adopted like any other rule which means the members must have an opportunity to comment prior to adoption and could by petition require a vote of the membership. Communications to the members with the reasons why the qualifications will result in a smoother running association is invaluable. To often the association is treated as a social organization with Board election being a recognition reward rather than the reality that the Board needs to be a multi-talented team that is running a major business. Any requirements must be reasonable and not discriminatory or create an image of an elitist controlling group.

## RECRUITING BOARD CANDIDATES

**QUESTION:** *We are having a more difficult time each year to get potential candidates to run for the Board, any suggestions?*

The best volunteers are usually recruited and a Nominating Committee is a good vehicle to use to encourage qualified residents to run for the Board or serve on an association committee. Many times good potential candidates are too modest to nominate themselves, but will respond to an invitation from a Nominating Committee. The Nominating Committee should have a charter indicating its number of members, the purpose and the selection criteria. Be sure to indicate if the role of Nominating Committee is just to solicit candidates or to actually recommend a slate of candidates. The Committee should be appointed at least six months prior to the election to permit plenty of time for the committee to solicit and screen candidates.

A Nominating Committee should not preclude anyone nominating themselves or being nominated by others. Residents need to be reminded in newsletters of the Board's role and importance in the operations of the Association. Although often regarded as a social organization, the Association is a business with the purpose of maintaining common area and enhancing the value of each home. Serving on the Board should be a satisfying experience, so continuing efforts should be made to provide Board training, short productive association meetings with appropriate staff support. Recognition is an essential element for attracting and retaining any volunteers, including Board members. Some suggested activities include: publishing names in newsletters; an annual recognition dinner; and recognition plaques for length of service or when leaving the Board.

## VOLUNTEER GUIDELINES

**QUESTION:** *How can we attract volunteers and keep them going in the right direction?*

Volunteers can be a great asset supplementing services and enhancing community involvement on almost any subject when properly directed and managed. Without clear guidelines and appropriate monitoring they can run amok and be a great frustration to the Board and themselves. The best volunteers are usually recruited – that is invited to work on specifically identified projects based on their background and experience. Committee members should be approved by the Board.

Before a committee or activity recruits volunteers, the Board should establish clear objectives and guidelines. The purpose or goals of the Committee should be stated and if it is to be an ad hoc or permanent committee. The guidelines should establish attendance requirements and how recommendations are to be forwarded to the Board, the relationship with staff and if there is to be a Board member liaison. Committee members should recognize that they are a recommending body and that the final decision may not be approved due to other considerations such as cost, timing or other matters with higher priorities. Some volunteers may actually be performing specific tasks that do not involve working as a committee. Activities such as citizen patrols, meals on wheels, neighbors checking on neighbors, etc., make for better communities, but volunteers must be reminded that others are depending upon them to be there and may require duplication of duties to assure that the responsibilities are being met. Insurance coverage can also be a major consideration that may require setting special requirements on volunteers.

Recognition is also an essential element for retaining volunteers. Some suggested activities include: publishing names in newsletters; an annual recognition dinner or party; providing an opportunity for reports at Board meetings; and recognition plaques for length of service.

## COMMITTEES

QUESTION: *How important are Committees and how do we attract and motivate volunteers to serve?*

The importance of recruiting qualified residents to run for the Board was previously covered in an earlier question and although many of the suggestions are also applicable to getting residents to serve on Committees, there may be substantially different motivations and criteria. Committees can be of great assistance to the Association by getting owners with experience and demonstrated talent involved. This may be particularly valuable to small associations that do not have professional staff.

A successful Committee starts with a written charter that clearly states the purpose and operating procedures of the Committee. The charter should indicate the number of members, terms, how recommendations will be presented to the Board and if the Committee is a permanent or limited objective Committee. It is recommended that there be attendance requirements, missing of a specified number of meetings in a year being considered a resignation. Committee members can be a good sounding board of the community as well as a buffer for the Board on controversial subjects.

As new owners come into the community, include a volunteer recruitment form in the New Owner Welcome packet. The form should have an optional request for personal background information on education, occupation or special interest areas and if they would be interested in serving on one or more of the described association committees. If there is a Welcome Committee a follow-up contact can be one of their responsibilities, or perhaps a call from a Board member or staff. A timely contact is essential.

Once you have selected Committee members there should be an orientation and opportunity for the volunteer to ask questions. It is also good to annually have a short meeting with each Committee and the Board to review their working relationship. Volunteers should be reminded that the association is a business with the purpose of maintaining common area and enhancing the value of each home. Committees need to be aware that the Board will be considering their recommendations in competition with other Committee projects and budget considerations. Serving on Committees should be a satisfying experience, so short productive meetings with appropriate professional support are desired.

Recognition is an essential element for attracting, motivating and retaining volunteers. Some suggested ways for thanking and recognizing volunteers include: publishing names in newsletters; an annual recognition dinner or event; and recognition plaques for length of service. Committee membership can also be a good stepping stone to the Board of Directors.

## COLLECTING DELINQUENT ASSESSMENTS
QUESTION: *Due to increasing delinquencies the Board for the first time is faced with instigating foreclosures, what should be our criteria or timing?*
The collection of assessments is an essential responsibility of the Board because uncollected funds will cause maintenance cutbacks or must be covered by the other owners. However, the recent downturn in real estate values coupled with lenders' excessive loan practices has left many delinquent properties with no equity. In some states the mortgage holder's liens are superior to the association lien and if that is the case the association foreclosure may be of no value. There may be exceptions where the delinquent property has equity because the delinquency is due to divorce or

other reasons not related to property values and thus each situation must be evaluated. A collection specialist will be able to make recommendations as to foreclosure feasibility and timing.

The first step in controlling delinquencies is the monthly monitoring of receipts and timely action to notify delinquent owners, adding late fees and where appropriate termination of privileges until payments are made current. The squeaking wheel gets the grease, so notification action may keep the association from being at the bottom of the list of monthly bills being paid. It is important that association liens be recorded, when permitted, to place the association's debt at as high a priority as possible should there be any equity in foreclosed property. Consider filing small claim court actions against delinquent owners; however any judgment still has the challenge of finding assets from which to obtain payment. Small Claims action is relatively inexpensive but can be time consuming.

Generally a delinquent association assessment owner is also not paying their mortgage, so the lender may already have started the foreclosure process. By monitoring the delinquency accounts and checking on the subject properties, a lack of landscape maintenance or even abandonment of the property is an indication of an emerging problem. Lenders who are foreclosing should be contacted in an attempt to build a relationship to assure that the property is secured and maintained to minimize the negative effect of foreclosed properties on the neighborhood. The association may want to consider providing basic yard maintenance or even turning on the water on vacant properties to keep landscaping alive. These are always controversial decisions and some attorneys do not support entering onto private property due to liability considerations.

## POLICE ENFORCEMENT

QUESTION: *Why won't police enforce traffic rules on our Association streets although we pay the same taxes is everyone else?*

This is a complex question with more than one possible answer. In general, public agencies do not feel they have a responsibility on private streets. Regarding who actually provides law enforcement services, in California, if you are in the unincorporated County, the California Highway Patrol provides traffic and accident enforcement with the Sheriff providing general law enforcement, but if you are in an incorporated City, City police provide both traffic and general law enforcement. If there is an accident, the CHP or City police will respond. In some cases, the City or CHP can provide traffic enforcement under special agreements with the Association. They generally will only enforce Vehicle Code violations and speed limits that comply with and are approved by the local public agency. This means striping and signing must comply with public standards and speed limits set in compliance with the vehicle code.

The Association may pay for enforcement service directly or in a few cases a Special Services District may be formed to collect a property tax to pay for the service. The local political attitude is a factor, so the first step should be to meet with the local police chief. Regular law enforcement personnel are substantially more expensive than private patrol but can also be more effective because violations are handled by the courts. When negotiating on the cost remember to get some credit for traffic fines that will go to the local agency.

## ASSESSMENT INCREASES

QUESTION: *What can the Board do to get owner support for necessary assessment increases or at least reduce negative rhetoric?*

It is only natural to hope that costs will never increase and it easy to be critical of those that must deal with the real world. The budget process that every Association goes through annually is the same process that a family budget must go through recognizing that regularly there are increases for supplies, utilities, insurance, etc. Throughout the year, residents need to be kept aware of the fact that certain costs are increasing so that it is not a surprise when the annual budget is adopted and key items are listed as costing more than the previous year.

Unfortunately many Boards will attempt to stay at the previous rate until a major increase is needed to meet current costs. Instead of increasing the justifiable cost of living at 2 or 3 percent each year, they wait until a 10 or 15% increase is necessary or even worse a special assessment is needed. The Board has a fiduciary duty to operate the association using good business judgment to maintain and enhance the community. It is not a popularity contest and often decisions are difficult, but remember to let the owners know why an increase is needed.

Governmental agencies continue to micro manage our industry in ways that also increase the cost of operations that ultimately must be passed on to owners. Several recent State legislations regarding rule change processing is a good example of something that sounds very democratic, but now requires many months to take simple actions at increased mailing and publication costs. Continuing communications of increased costs for the Association through newsletters, inserts in billings or other notices, use of a web page, owner forums and other means are excellent tools. The best rule is "no surprises".

## BID SHOPPING
QUESTION: *What is meant by "bid shopping" and is it beneficial?*
Associations go out for bids on a variety of contracts, some of which are one time projects, such as new construction, while other contracts may be long term relationships, such as landscape maintenance and

security. Bids may be solicited through open or informal processes or by closed or sealed bids. Informal bids are usually solicited by personal contacts with bids received via email, fax or letter at any time. Sealed bids are usually solicited from detailed specifications and bids must be received at a specific time in a sealed envelope so all bids will be opened at the same time. In either process, after the bids are reviewed, the low bidder is determined based on meeting the specifications, experience, references and the ability to successfully perform the work. Some organizations have a policy of only accepting the lowest bid, which is not recommended because price is only one component of a successful contract.

"Bid Shopping" is the practice of taking the low bid from either of the two above described processes, and then contacting the other bidders to see if they will lower their bids. Some Boards feel this is a good method to get the best possible price and frankly it is usually possible to get a lower price on most things if you don't care about quality, performance or what kind of image your association will have with vendors.

*Association's reputation with vendors has value.* When vendors find their bids are being "shopped", they will cease to bid on future projects or only submit high prices. Associations with a negative reputation will also find itself on the bottom of the priority list when there are emergencies or area wide problems such as roof leaks in the rain or other emergency repairs when there are many calls and limited personnel or equipment available. It costs vendors time and money to prepare competitive bids and they deserve to be treated fairly and honestly.

Associations should also be realistic in bid result expectations. Most good contractors are willing to provide unit cost estimates or by checking with other association managers who have been through similar bidding, a realistic bid expectation can be anticipated. If bids come in far above estimates check your specifications to see if there is something affecting the cost that can be changed. The objective of the bidding process is to obtain quality work at a fair price to both the buyer and the vendor.

## WORKERS COMPENSATION INSURANCE

QUESTION: *Why should our association carry workers compensation insurance when we do not have employees and require our contractors to have insurance?*

An association should carry workers compensation liability insurance to protect against exposure from claims by injured workers employed by an uninsured or unlicensed contractor who may be working on association property. Court cases continue to go against the property owner from injured workers working on site even when not employees of the owner. Insurance fees are usually minimal when there are no employees because they are based on actual payroll. Even a good system by the Association to pre-qualify contractors can have someone slip through or are not a guarantee that a contractor's insurance may be cancelled without notice to the Association. We all know that hiring an unlicensed and uninsured contractor is never a good idea and a small savings can end up being very costly. Yet it is regularly done.

Another exposure of concern may be contractors' employees operating vehicles on association property. Require verification that all contractor employees driving onto the property have a driver's license and vehicle insurance coverage.

I personally am aware of two incidents that cost thousands of dollars in legal fees. In one case, as part of a facility redecoration, a drapery company was contracted to provide carpet and drapes and they intern subcontracted with a drapery installer who fell off a latter and broke his arm. He did not have insurance and sued the property owner rather than the drapery company that hired him. Although he did not win, the case lasted four years and cost thousands in legal fees. In another case, in order to save money an association did major construction as an owner/builder project and designated the contractor as an employee of the Association for the project. An employee was hurt during the construction and cost the association substantially more than the "savings" of using an insured licensed contractor.

Due to increasing litigation, many Associations have raised their liability insurance requirements for all contractors, which may eliminate many good small contractors who can not obtain multimillion dollar coverage. An alternative may be to have a sliding scale insurance requirement that sets a lower minimum insurance for small specialized jobs.

## DIRECTORS & OFFICERS INSURANCE

QUESTION: *The Board is having a problem getting D&O insurance because a Board member is suing the association, what should we do?* This is a complex question that will need professional guidance for the Board to assure that the "good business judgment" rule is being followed. Having adequate insurance coverage is a fiduciary responsibility and without D&O coverage Board members could be at personal risk. Frankly, I would never serve on a Board without D&O coverage.

An insurance broker specializing in HOA coverage and legal council should be the primary sources for guidance on insurance coverage. In some cases, it may not be possible to obtain insurance coverage or the coverage may be unreasonably expensive or have an excessive deductible. By documenting that reasonable alternatives have been explored and then informing the membership of the final choices, the Board can demonstrate that they have preformed their fiduciary duties. Certain activities may not be undertaken due to the cost or lack of adequate insurance available to protect the Association.

## RESERVE FUNDS

QUESTION: *How much money should be in an Association's Reserve Fund? Can a Board of Directors opt not to maintain a Reserve Fund?*

An Association Reserve Fund is an orderly savings from member assessments to handle expected maintenance and unanticipated emergencies. Some states' laws require that the Board of Directors for every Association with common area facilities must cause to be conducted a study to identify all major common area components, the remaining useful life, the estimated cost to repair or replace and the reserve funds available. The Board should include in the annual budget report a summary of the Association's Reserve Study and the percentage funded. There may also be additional requirements in the Association's CC&Rs. When the law or CC&Rs does not set a minimum funding requirement, it is my opinion that over 75% is desired and that under 50% is dangerously low.

There are various methods of calculating the total reserve needs and the method used should be described in the Reserve Study and disclosed to members. Regarding not maintaining a Reserve fund, the Board has a fiduciary responsibility to comply with applicable Law unless the Association members have voted otherwise and that information is regularly disclosed to members. Reserves studies deal with determining long range maintenance and availability of funds to prevent unexpected assessments which could result in owners on limited income from being forced out of their homes. Lack of adequate funding for reserves can also negatively impact property values, home loans and the ability to sell property in the development. In addition to a desired independent review every three years, the Board should annually review the Reserve Study and report to the members.

## BUILDING RESERVE FUNDS

QUESTION: *Our Association Reserves are substantially under funded and they never seem to improve, what can be done without increasing our assessments which are already high?*

Building reserves is very much like planning for retirement or building a nest egg available for major expenditures. Although there may not be set requirements for funding, the Board has a fiduciary responsibility for having the financial ability to maintain the Association's assets. Lack of reserves may impact the value of homes in the development or require unpopular special assessments that cause unexpected hardships. When reserves are not adequately funded, a long range plan should be implemented to correct the problem and be communicated to the owners. Owners need to be reminded that reserves are a saving account to meet anticipated future needs.

Following are ways to build reserves:
First, the regular assessment should include designated funds that will ultimately fund the reserves. The time period to make up deficiencies must be realistic. When owners indicate that assessments are already too high without reserve funding they are being unrealistic, because if they can not afford a monthly contribution, how will they handle a large special assessment to fund repairs or replacements?

Second, adequately funded reserves will also help generate funds through their investment. However, there should be an investment policy which should not risk principal.

Third, monthly contributions to the reserves should not be siphoned off by using reserve funds for handling operating fund shortages. In a tight budget it can be tempting to charge routine maintenance expenses to the reserves, which defeats the necessary build up of funds.

Forth, any budget surplus at the end of the year can be transferred to reserves to improve an under funded situation.

There are differing views as to what is an appropriate percentage for reserve fund balances. In my opinion, it depends on the type of assets covered by the reserves. In a condominium, where roofs, plumbing and other essential maintenance is necessary for living units, the percentage has to be higher than for a PUD where the improvements may be pools or aesthetic elements that can be shut down if funds are not available. Generally, reserves under 50% funding may be considered under funded, around 75% is considered adequate, and of course funding approaching 100% is the goal.

## SELLING COMMON AREA AMENITIES

QUESTION: *Can an Association close down amenities and sell common area to balance the budget or fund necessary repairs?*

Unfortunately this question is becoming more common as facilities age and reserves for repairs and replacement were not adequately funded. Although facilities may be underused, their closure may impact the development's image and ultimately individual property values. Any possible closure of amenities should be publicized to all owners and there be opportunities for owners to comment or even vote prior to any action. An option may be to generate income by opening amenities to non members, although caution is advised because the projected income may be offset by costs, owner opposition or wear and tear to the facilities.

Selling common area may also be restricted by the recorded Association Covenants, in addition to State Law. First check your documents, State regulations and local zoning or subdivision requirement that permitted the development. Although there are a few exceptions, I doubt if any significant revenue can be generated without an affirmative vote of the owners, which is very difficult to achieve. An additional problem may be governmental zoning for any change in use. Many associations are Planned Unit Developments or special use permits, changes to which are very costly and time consuming.

Funding shortages for repairs or replacements is most often concentrated in older developments that may have never considered having Reserve funding. The unrealistic perception that assessments will not increase as the development ages is part of the problem, when the reality is that major assessment increases will be needed to repair, remodel and in some cases totally rebuild as facilities become obsolete. Boards have a fiduciary responsibility to communicate to owners these realities.

## INVESTING HOA FUNDS

QUESTION: *Some of our members feel we should be getting a larger return on our reserves and other excess funds by investing in the Stock Market, where do most associations invest their funds?*
The Board must never forget that they are fiduciaries, must use sound business judgment and administer the Associations funds on behalf of ALL the owners. First the governing documents should be checked to see if there are requirements on how association funds can be invested. Then it would be appropriate for the Board to create and adopt an investment policy on which owners may comment.

There are three general issues to be prioritized in any investment policy: 1. Safety or preservation of capital; 2. Yield or return; and 3. Liquidity or availability. A lesser concern may be the complexity or convenience of handling of the investments. Once the decision is made as to what are the association's investment priorities, each type of investment can be readily evaluated.

In my opinion, capital should always be at minimum risk. Thus the safest investment would be accounts backed by the government, such as Certificates of Deposit (CDs) to a maximum of $100,000 per institution. At times $100,000 investment interest is slightly higher than lesser amounts, so in order for the income to be guaranteed it would need to be paid monthly because if left in the account the interest would exceed the limit of the bank's guarantee insurance. Since this is income rather than the original capital I feel this could be considered a reasonable business decision. Several investment services have programs that will distribute an Association's investments among several banks in order to preserve the government guarantees with only one signature card, which is a great convenience. Some of the larger investment companies also have private insurance as a guarantee, which in my opinion is not the same as government guarantees.

Bonds and Securities if kept for the term of the Bond or Security may be appropriate if the funds will not be needed prior to that date. Their value may fluctuate during the ensuing period and have a loss if they are cashed in early.

Stocks or mutual funds in the long run have generally a higher return than CDs; however there is greater risk since the value may fluctuate daily. I do not recommend stock investing. The simple fact is that profit and risk are related. The greater the return, the greater the risk.

There are several other types of investments, ranging from low interest short term investment accounts, US Treasuries, institutional funds and other equities. Another issue may be the question of investing in Tax Exempt instruments, depending on your corporate tax type. Each should be evaluated based on the previously suggested priorities; safety, liquidity and yield. Whatever the Board decides to do, it should be communicated to the members.

As a factual matter, newer associations appear to have adequately funded reserves, while the older associations with the greatest financial needs are the least funded. This is because newer associations started funding at their inception before they had to make expenditures. Older associations are often unrealistic concerning the replacement and modernization of improvements and are trying to maintain unrealistic low assessments. Reserves funding is an investment to meet future needs, both anticipated and unexpected.

## FURNISHING LEGAL DOCUMENTS

QUESTION: *We are a small association and want to know if we are responsible for providing HOA documents to new buyers?*

The Association is only responsible to its members (current owners in title) to provide documents and information. The seller may be required to provide full disclosure to the buyer about the property, which would include HOA documents and various Association disclosures. So indirectly the HOA may be providing the material that the seller needs to provide the buyer, and may charge a fee to cover the cost of that service. Your CC&Rs are recorded documents so the title company may be providing them to the escrow. Also there are special services that provide the documents at reduced costs. The escrow will make a demand on the Association for the current assessment balance of the seller's account so it can be prorated at close of escrow and a transfer fee charged to cover the Association's costs. If contracting with a management company, they may be handling these matters and charging the escrow for the costs.

Every effort should be made to have the Association's CC&Rs, Bylaws and copies of the rules given to all potential buyers to avoid future problems. Some states also require, and it is good business, to provide copies of the Association budget, Reserve study and minutes of the Board meetings. An informed buyer will be a more positive and supportive member.

## EMPLOYEE VERSUS MANAGEMENT COMPANIES
QUESTION: *Can hiring a Management Company and discharging HOA employees lower the monthly assessments, as advocated by some members?*
This is a complex issue involving more than just immediate costs. Obviously the size and complexity of the Association is a factor. Also management/personnel are only a portion of the operating costs for an Association. "Outsourcing" has become a more common way of doing business as the increased complexity of governmental regulations, litigation and personnel rules require specialized skills that can not always be available to smaller organizations. Members on both sides of the debate, somehow think that all the employees can be replaced instantly by a management company, but that just doesn't happen. In some cases, the staff is absorbed into the pool of management company employees and trained in their procedures. Sometimes employees are directly reimbursable, with other services included in a lump sum monthly fee.

Management Companies can have several advantages and cost savings, where staff is shared with other associations such as

Finance, Contacting, Human Resources, Training and Technology. By sharing costs and being part of larger organization, better quality employees may be able to be attracted and retained. The down side can be employee loyalty – is it to the association or the management company? The Association will be expected to adapt to the management company's standardized procedures. Staffing may be changed at will by the management company. Also should the Board decide to a change of management companies, it can be very difficult and result in a loss of record continuity and historical reference.

The choice is not just an either or decision. There can be a blended organization of employees and out sourced services, with the Board of Directors hiring an on-site manager with a small key staff and contracting for basic services, such as finance and accounting, IT, or such services as landscaping, maintenance and security. There can be a cost benefit to contracting based on scale and flexibility. In my opinion the trend will continue to be towards more out sourcing.

## CHANGING MANAGEMENT COMPANIES

QUESTION: *What are the major considerations in the Board changing management or major contract services?*

The question does not indicate the reason for change, which will be a factor in listing the considerations of how the change is handled. Loss of continuity, historical records and informal procedures may be a consequence of any change. It the motivation for a change is just to save money, the results may be a reduction in quality of service. It is almost always possible to get a lower price on any service, which in the long run may be more costly or result in residents' complaints due to an expectation of better service when there is actually a reduction.

Any new contract will require a "learning curve" for a new service provider and there may be difficulties in continuity, historical records, warrantees or litigation information. If the change is prompted by a perceived decline in quality of service or on site personnel, the situation should have been discussed with the current contractor prior to going out for bids to provide an opportunity to identify and correct the problems. Often a new Board runs for election on the basis of changing contractors when they have limited knowledge about the scope of the contract or realistic related costs. It sounds like it is easy to just replace the contractor or on site personnel, but this is not always the case and may just lead to new problems.

When the decision has been made to change service contractors, meet with the principals and agree upon transition timing. Except in cases of illegal acts, contractors will desire an orderly transfer of responsibilities, records and bank accounts. All records of the Association are Association property and can not be held hostage, and payments due the contractor should also not be withheld. It doesn't pay to "burn bridges" by either party because the reputation of all is at risk. Often the Association may desire to return to a previous contractor and our profession is relatively small, so how the situation is handled will reflect on the reputation of both parties for future business. The same issue may apply to discharging on site personnel, particularly if a long time employee. A severance package may to cheaper than negative publicity, member involvement or potential litigation. Any new contract bidding should begin with detailed professionally prepared specifications.

## PROFESSIONAL DESIGNATIONS
QUESTION: *What is the meaning or value of the letters following many association managers' names, such as CPM, CMCA, CCAM, MCM, PCAM, etc.?*

The capital letters following a manager's name stand for professional designations that have been achieved through education or experience. Unfortunately it has become an "alphabet" soup because of the number of organizations having designations and the differing requirements. Just as in a college education, there is an AA Degree, which usually takes about two years, the BA Degree about four years and an MA taking five or six years. The professional designations may be relatively simple and only take a few hours of classes or may take hundreds of hours or several years.

The most common Community Association Institute (CAI) designations are the CMCA, an entry level designation, the AMS which indicates completion of a basic association management course, with the PCAM being the most comprehensive, requiring completion of several courses, professional involvement and a case study. The LSM designation is for large scale on-site managers. In California, there is a managers' organization, California Association of Community Managers (CACM), which has a CCAM designation that requires completion of four short core courses and an ethics class. There is a national on-site managers' organization, Community Managers International Association (CMIA) that has an MCM designation based on experience coupled with minimum educational requirements. The Institute of Real Estate Management (IREM) is a national real estate association that has the CPM designation, similar to the PCAM, that has been obtained by many association managers, although more common for commercial real estate management. The CMAA is an association for club managers that have food and beverage operations and have designations for their members who may also be managing an HOA.

In addition to education and experience requirements, many of the designations also have ethics codes that must be adhered to as well as continuing educational course work. This summary has only briefly highlighted the requirements to obtain or maintain the listed designations and the individual organizations should be contacted to determine specific requirements. By obtaining the designations, managers are demonstrating their desire to improve their skills as well as striving to develop higher standards for HOA professionals.

## RECRUITING EMPLOYEES

QUESTION: *What are the best sources for recruiting personnel and determining appropriate salaries?*

The type of personnel has not been indicated, but there is competition for professional experienced employees in most areas. In addition to the normal sources, such as newspaper advertising and the State Department of Employment, there are specialized sources available to homeowner associations. CAI has on its website at: caionline.org, a "Careers Center" section. Under "Careers" there is a "Job Bank" section with a "Job Listings" category for posting job openings, as well as a "Resumes" category for those looking for positions. Under Jobs and Resumes there are categories for "administrative assistant", "financial", "maintenance", "on-site", "human resources", "portfolio manager" and "technician". This CAI service is provided at no cost. The internet also offers numerous recruitment sites.

There are "headhunter" services available, two of which are former managers, Julie Adamen and Robb Felix. Contracting for soliciting and screening of applications by personnel consultants is worth considering, particularly for on-site managers for large Associations. Screening of applications not only requires skill but there are many legal limitations on what information can be requested, and if violated could be source of discrimination litigation. When there are numerous applications from a variety of backgrounds, Boards can be overwhelmed with the screening details when their attentions should be concentrated on determining the final selection. Possibly the most important step in recruiting is a clear description of the job and the Board having a consensus on the most important traits desired. Do not forget to check references and in some top management cases it may be worth visiting the applicant's current employment association.

Having a competitive salary is important for attracting and keeping quality employees. Although there are national salary surveys, it is generally a local issue related to area cost of living. Developing a relationship and sharing information with other associations in your area is a good source for current salary rates. Business associations such as the Chamber of Commerce also publish salaries for some categories. Salaries should be reviewed annually along with the annual price index factors to remain competitive. Often it is only after employees leave and the association is unable to attract replacements that salaries are raised. Employee turnover is expense to an association, not only monetary but in continuity and disruptive services to owners.

## GIFT POLICY
QUESTION: *Is there an industry standard for acceptable holiday gifts from vendors or members?*
This is an issue that needs to be regularly reviewed since it could reflect on the image, both real and perceived, of the Association, employees and Board members. Certified managers have a standard of ethics that addresses gifts and they can lose their designation for violations. Non-certified managers and other employees need guidance through a Board adopted policy.

Generally acceptable gifts are those given to the office as whole, such as providing deserts, an office luncheon or a donation to a favored charity. Gifts from residents to select employees, such as landscapers or golf starters should be discouraged because it implies they may be receiving special treatment. It also is unfair because the employees in regular contact with members are part of a team that should be recognized and treated equally. In the case of a golf course, the pro or starter may have the daily contact, but it is the crew residents rarely see that do the work that keeps the course in good condition. Some members are very generous while others feel employee compensation is sufficient. An alternative method is to include a suggested optional holiday donation on one of the monthly assessment billings for employee recognition and then distribute it on a predetermined formula. In some cases it is equally divided or weighted based on length of service or other criteria. We are in a competitive society and it would be appropriate to see what other area, similar associations are doing.

Board members must remember they have a fiduciary responsibility that should not be influenced by vendor gifts. Probably the most important rule is to publicly disclose the source and extent of any gifts received.

## STATE LAW PREEMPTION
QUESTION: *What can Board members/staff do to discourage State law makers from making managing Associations more difficult?*
Several State Legislatures continue to react to individual complaints against a homeowner association by writing laws that penalize all associations or just add a lot of extra work and costs. Although several related professional organizations have advocacy groups, individual voters developing personal relationships with their State representatives can be of great value in communicating our side

of the story. CAI, through CLAC, CACM and ECHO regularly provide positive information about homeowner associations but are continuously under attack by a small group of anti-HOA individuals. Also the media regularly distorts or sensationalizes negative stories involving allegations by individuals against their Associations.

Most new developments are in Homeowner Associations because local governments do not want to pay for new streets, landscaping, parks and recreation facilities. At the same time, some Legislatures make it more difficult for Boards to enforce their rules, more costly to conduct their elections and often preempt association documents and operating procedures. Legislature members do not often understand associations but treat them as semi-government entities. The problem is associations do not have the authority or legal protections of government.

Association members can be very influential by getting to know their locally elected officials and their district staffs. During a recent discussion with a former Legislator, he indicated that personal letters and calls from his District voters did get greater attention than a volume of form letters and mass emails. He indicated that form letters were usually responded to by form letters, whereby personal letters from District voters received personal responses. Invitations to a "Candidates Night" during elections, or a "Meet Your Elected Representative" at the Association clubhouse or in a member's home can be an excellent way to build a relationship. When the Association is in need of assistance it will be easier for an elected official to say "Yes" and more difficult to say "No" to a friend. Positive relationships need to be cultivated and built prior to the need. Don't forget to visit and get to know the local staff by regularly visiting the District Office of the elected representatives.

## UNANTICIPATED CHANGES

**QUESTION:** *Handling the unexpected, such as the loss of key personnel?*

In California we are regularly reminded of the potential dangers and damage from earthquakes that may occur without advanced warning, and in fact almost every State has potential for emergencies from flooding, hurricanes, tornados, or fire and should have insurance and emergency reaction plans. But what about loss of key personnel? I have generally been affiliated with larger associations, which have experienced staff to draw on, but still there may be immediate problems, important projects delayed and items falling through the cracks. Consider some of the following to minimize the negative effect of the unexpected absence of key employees:

BINDER WORKBOOK for each position which contains an outline of duties, schedule of events with deadlines, contacts and forms;

CROSS TRAINING for all key positions with partnered employees able and expecting to step in to fill any voids;

RECRUITING SERVICE active relationship established before there is a need, which can be informal and is particularly important for smaller organizations and could include providing temporary staffing;

MAINTAIN RELATIONSHIPS with nearby managers or similar size associations, as well as CAI; and

SUPPORT ANNUAL PHYSICALS for key employees.

## MEMBER DISPUTES

**QUESTION:** *When should a Board or Association staff get involved in a dispute between two owners?*

Although the intentions may be good this is an activity that should be approached with great caution and anyone involved should be knowledgeable on the role of a mediator. Another consideration must be a careful look at the CC&Rs and the Board's mission statement on the role of the Association because involvement could have legal consequences that result in expenses or claims against the D&O insurance for the Board exceeding its proper role.

That being said, the Association may provide guidance to owners by listening to the individuals and encouraging those involved to talk directly to each other. Many times venting to a sympatric listener will help defuse the problem. My assumption is that the issues involved in this question are civil rather than a violation of the CC&Rs and that is why the owners must deal directly with each other. The Association can provide general reference material such as listing local mediation service providers, addresses for City/County offices that may have information on common conflict subjects, providing tract maps or other related public documents and forms such as Small Claims Court procedures. The Association projects a better image if a referral can be made or general information provided rather than responding that it is not an association issue and thus can not get involved.

When disputes get to a point what may require the cost of a mediator expert witness or attorney, disputing owners would like to get the Association in the middle to do the work and pick up the costs. With any information provided or personal involvement it must be regularly made clear that the Association is only providing assistance as a courtesy and not as a substitute for the services of an attorney or other professionals. Although Associations have procedures for enforcing the CC&Rs and rules, in most cases compliance with the rules is achieved through diplomacy rather than litigation due to the cost and time it takes.

## OMBUDSMAN

QUESTION: *Is there a "Homeowners' Advocate" or "Ombudsman" to protect our rights and property against negligent Boards of Directors?*

There currently is no State HOA Ombudsman in California although the State Legislature has been considering establishing such a State agency. Some states have consumer protection departments, usually under the Real Estate regulatory agencies. The negative side of creating a new State agency is that the costs of such a service will most likely be a charged to all Associations and there will be difficulty in defining what authority the Ombudsman would have to override actions of elected Board members, fine or even take over the Association's operations. Homeowner Associations are in some ways similar to local governments in that the members elect a Board of Directors to manage the association and enforce the agreements that were created by the developer. Every owner has the right to attend all meetings, inspect the records and finances of the association. The Board must operate with the recorded CC&Rs, as well as State laws regulating Common Interest Developments and in most cases the State Corporation Code, as Associations are generally incorporated.

It was not indicated what specific items of "negligence" by the Board was the issue. If the owners do not feel the Board is appropriately handling the affairs of the Association, owners should run for the Board or express their concerns by attending and participating in Board meetings. Often the problem may be that the Board is not keeping the members informed concerning Board actions or the financial condition of the Association. There may be members unhappy that the Board is not doing enough to maintain the property or enforce their covenants. On the opposite side are those who think the assessments are too high and the Board is too aggressive in rules enforcement. The Board should be striving to determine community consensus while complying with applicable law and Association documents. The challenge is that Boards' often do not communicate adequate information to their members.

State laws continues to increase the Association's responsibility to give advanced notice to the members on the budget, assessment changes, audits, funding for Reserves, Board meeting notices and how elections are conducted. Often the members most critical of the Board are unwilling to take the time to participate or serve on the Board or Committees.

Some States, such as Nevada, have established an Ombudsman State Agency with a Commission that may investigate and penalize Board members and managers, the cost which is assessed against Associations. It has also increased educational requirements for Board members and managers. It will be interesting to see if the process will improve or have a negative impact on Association operations. New laws are often a reaction to an isolated problem, but impact all associations and are written to empower the individual member. The Legislature usually does not appear to recognize the financial impact due to new regulations that result in higher monthly fees to the homeowners. The recent California regulations on rule changes and election processing are good examples of adding substantial administrative costs to every Association.

## MEMBER DIRECTORIES
QUESTION: *What are the benefits or problems in an association printing a directory of HOA members and what information should or should not be included?*

This is an issue that is a good subject for a survey to determine the member's support for having a directory of all owners. A directory is a good tool towards building neighborhood relationships. It can also be of value during emergencies or unexpected situations when members may need to contact neighbors when association staff is not available.

California State law now permits any owner to request and obtain Association membership lists for other than commercial uses. The law does permit members to opt out of the mailing list provided by the Association. However, the State mandated Association membership mailing list usually only contains the address and property legal ownership name, which may even be a trust or corporation.

An Association published directory may provide substantially more information than that required by State law, such as including family member names, phone numbers and may be cross indexed by address as well as last names. A form should be circulated in advance to all owners asking for the information proposed to be included in the directory, including giving the option to be "unlisted".

The type of directory will be influenced by the size of the association, ranging from simple stapled copies to attractive binders. A three ring binder is most desirable so that updated pages can be inserted. Other items such as important phone numbers, Board and Committee memberships, regular meeting times and general association rules and regulations may also be included.

The issue of having advertising to fund the cost of a Directory or perhaps even to generate a profit can be a consideration. Although advertising is not generally recommended for association directories or newsletters by CAI, it can be of benefit to owners in large gated associations where businesses that desire to provide services to residents do not have access to the area.

Although most Associations may only think of their responsibility as being the maintenance and enhancement of Association property, don't under estimate the positive effect of directories in facilitating neighbors getting to know each other and fostering a sense of community.

## PRESS RELATIONS

QUESTION: *Can newspaper reporters attend Board meeting and who should deal with the press regarding Board business?*

Press or TV reporters do not have the right to attend Association meetings, only the members have the right to attend. Some Boards do invite guests, including the press when there are subjects of community interest, but this would be a policy decision of the Board. Unfortunately the press is usually looking for sensationalism and is generally not necessarily interested in projecting a positive image of the Association. That being said, there can be value in building a positive relationship with the press so that they will have a contact in the Association to obtain factual information before writing articles. It is also an opportunity to educate reporters on the role of the Association, and exactly what authority is in the documents and the limits to that authority.

Critics within the Association will feed negative information to reporters or write letters to the editor so you need to establish a contact with whom a trusting relationship can be developed. This is particularly important if there is a newspaper or TV station that regularly covers your area. It is usually easy to maintain a contact with the press because they normally have a reporter assigned to specific areas. TV is more difficult because they want instant responses and will use whoever is in the area. TV crews will also film a lengthy session that the editor may bring down to less than a minute, so be careful on interviews because only a few words out of context may be shown.

The Board should designate a spokesman to speak for the Association so that there is continuity and not conflicting information being circulated. There is nothing wrong with saying, "I don't know the answer, but I will find out and get back to you". Most important, get back to the reporter quickly and remember they have publication deadlines.

Associations have not done the best job in communicating with the public while our critics have regularly exploited negative incidents. A few years ago the national TV program "20-20" had a special that was totally one sided against homeowner associations. As a result of such negative publicity and continuing efforts by critics, State Legislatures continue to write laws negatively impacting Association by increasing costs and limiting the ability operate effectively. Surveys show that the vast majority of HOA residents are happy with how their Associations operate but this is not what the press continues to publicize.

## DELINQUENT MEMBER INFORMATION
QUESTION: *How can someone find out whom and how many owners are delinquent in their assessment payments to an association?*
Information on the Association's delinquent accounts could be an important consideration for a potential buyer or a lender. However, information concerning individual owners is restricted by privacy laws and because Associations are private corporations, access to records are limited to members (owners). When there is a difficult real estate market and increased mortgage defaults, the stability of property ownership in a development and information on the financial strength of the association could be a major concern.

## MEMBER ONLY ACCESS
Only the property owner (member) of an association has a right to access to association records. There are even privacy concerns with giving out the names of delinquent owners to members and thus delinquent accounts are usually only identified by account numbers. The Board of Directors regularly reviews monthly delinquency reports

that indicate late payment percentages and they may act to instigate recording liens and ultimately foreclosure. A potential buyer or lender may request the seller of a unit to provide a copy of the Association budget, financial statements and Board meeting minutes which should be some indication of the financial condition of the Association, with the minutes indicating Board motions on filing liens or foreclosure actions. Any liens filed will be public record and accessible.

## OWNER DISCLOSURES

A seller or owner is required to disclose all information they are aware of concerning the property and the Association, in addition to providing specific Association documents and Board minutes. Local realtors with listings in the development could also be a good source for information on properties in foreclosure or previously sold through foreclosure.

## DELINQUENCY PROCESS

In California, State law has set requirements for notice, process and time periods for filing association liens and instigating foreclosure. Delinquent assessments must exceed $1,800 or be more than 12 months overdue before an association may use judicial or nonjudicial foreclosure. The Association must have a written policy statement for collecting delinquent assessments and must distribute that statement to all owners annually. Other states may have specific requirements in addition to the process covered in the CC&Rs. There is often a mixed view about the Board aggressively working to collect delinquent accounts, but owners must understand that this is a fiduciary responsibility of the Board to protect the financial condition of the Association. By the same token, delinquent owners should communicate with the Association when they can not pay their assessments in some cases to possibly delay foreclosure action and minimize collection costs by negotiating a payment plan or sale period.

# FIGHT OR FLIGHT

QUESTION: *What criteria should be considered when determining whether to "Fight, Flight or Litigate?*

Every situation or conflict must be evaluated on a variety of factors including ethical, moral, financial, precedence and legal considerations as well as the overall importance when looking at the "big picture". Too often egos or the obsession of proving that one party is "right" has become the dominate force. The threat and intimidation of litigation continues to complicate developing logical and reasonable solutions rather than escalating disputes.

Whether it is a homeowner wanting their way or a Board enforcing the CC&Rs, too often a minor conflict escalates into complex time consuming and costly conflicts. The first criteria should be to deal with situations as rapidly as possible rather than letting them fester. The Board should authorize staff or if volunteer driven, designate specific Board members with the authority to gather facts and develop alternative solutions. Although legal counsel may be consulted, it has been my experience that having lawyers handle the problem is not productive unless the problem has major liability ramifications. If the issue involves technical issues such as engineering use an independent third party.

If the decision has been made to "fight", present your case to the other party in a courteous professional manner based on sharing facts and avoiding emotions. Offering mediation or arbitration can be an effective alternative. This decision may also mean the Board does not do anything but leaves it to the other party to take action. A problem may disappear when the complaining party finds the cost to instigate litigation and the time and risks involved.

If the decision has been made to capitulate to the situation (flight), do it graciously and clarify in the Association records why the decision has been and what precedence, if any, is being set. If the decision is to "litigate", the potential cost should be estimated and if existing legal counsel or a special counsel is needed. If has been my experience that legal costs have greatly exceeded estimates and even when you win, often it has been so costly, with the only real winners being the attorneys on both sides. Also the State Legislature continues to make it difficult for homeowner associations to recover legal costs.

The above comments are very general and subjective because each issue must be evaluated on its own merits and implications. I would expect some attorneys and other experienced managers might express a different approach, but all would agree that every effort should be made to determine the facts before any decision is made.

## MEETING PRESENTATIONS
QUESTION: *How can a homeowner be effective in addressing or influencing the Board of Directors?*
Most meetings of the Board of Directors are open to all members and there is usually a designated time at each meeting for members to address the Board on any subject. The method and attitude of the presentation will probably determine the effectiveness.

## BE RESPECTFUL
First, be aware that the Board members are neighbors who have volunteered to serve on the Board and deserve to be treated respectfully and courteously. Presentations usually have time limits because the purpose of Board meetings is to conduct the business of the Corporation

and is not a public forum. Thus be brief and specific. The annual meeting of the Association or a public forum meeting will usually include greater member participation. Also personal attacks or threats are not effective and detract from the subject being presented. Also don't attack enforcement personnel who may just be doing their jobs.

## WRITTEN BACKUP MATERIAL

Submission of written backup material at least two weeks prior to the meeting is recommended so that it can be included in the Board agenda material. The agenda and backup material are usually given to the Board several days prior to the meeting, so don't wait to give it out at the meeting. It is wise to bring extra copies in case the material was not distributed or the Board member forgot to bring their copies. Presentations should be brief and factual with exhibits, where appropriate.

## NO SHORTCUTS

On any problem or issue be sure that you have attempted to solve the problem thru normal channels before going to the Board. Was the issue discussed with Association staff or appropriate Sub-Committees of the Board before going to the Board? Challenging architectural rules by attempting to bypass the Architectural Committee will complicate the problem.

## ALTERNATIVES/COMPROMISE

Most problems may have more than one solution, and although you may request a specific action, be open to discussing alternatives or a compromise. This is particularly true with architectural matters where sometimes a design change can meet the CC&Rs and permit the requested approval. If a compromise is approved be sure to abide by the change and not attempt to bootleg the denied design.

## REALISTIC EXPECTATIONS

Do not expect the Board to immediately act on requests that are brought up during public comment periods. Most Boards will want to review information and may be concerned with precedence or legal ramifications. State law may also limit the Board's ability to act on items that are not agenda items. Also remember there are two sides to every story.

## BECOME A PARTICIPANT

Major subjects such as the Association budget, assessments, changing rules, etc., can take a great deal of time and study. Attend Board meetings and get involved by volunteering to serve on committees or even run for the Board. Talk with neighbors and get their views. However don't assume that because neighbors do not challenge your comments that they agree with you. Often neighbor do not want to offend or get involved in controversies. It is your Association, get involved but remember the Board is there to do what is best for the community, not necessarily pleasing to each individual.

## NEIGHBORHOOD FEUDS

QUESTION: *What is the best approach to handling neighborhood feuds?*

One of the more frustrating challenges for association managers and board members is dealing with feuding neighbors. Often neighbors who have never spoken will become chronic generators of complaints that waste staff or volunteers' time that would have probably never developed if the residents were just civil to each other. Often the complaints to the association do not deal with the real issues or the complainants are not being honest. Following are examples of unreasonable neighbors:

## CROWING ROOSTERS

A resident called the Association office complaining about a neighbor raising chickens. She indicated that they were close friends with the neighbor and did not want their name used as a complainant. When the neighbor was contacted, they indicated that they did not raise chickens, but her elementary school son had a rooster that had been kept from a school project. She wanted to know who the complainant was, because "her neighbors loved the rooster". She then made the wrong assumption that the complainant was the elderly lady across the street and began to make complaints about the elderly lady's house.

It is a good policy to not disclose the complainant's name, but it is also important not to start another feud when the wrong person is blamed. In this case it was important to go back to the original complainant and suggest that they tell their neighbor that the rooster crowing was a problem. It is also wise to get complaints such as this in writing when they can not be readily observed by Association representatives from common area.

## BILLBOARD IN REAR YARD

A call to the Association questioned if there was a restriction on billboards in a rear yard? It was indicated that all signs needed approval and billboards were not permitted. The complainant indicated there was one in his neighbor's rear yard. In checking, a large sign was observed stating "Keep your hands off my fruit tree". In speaking with both parties, it was indicated they had never met or spoke to each other. The issue was that a limb of the fruit tree hung over into the neighbor's patio and the neighbor felt he had the right to pick the fruit that was over his property. It was indicated to both parties that it was ridicules that they had not spoken to each other on the subject and that the Association would not get involved in what was a civil matter that should not be a problem for reasonable people. The solution was not sign regulations, but an understanding between the neighbors about tree limbs extending over property lines and the courtesy to speak to neighbors before cutting off tree limbs or picking fruit from a tree that does not belong to you. This would also apply to the tree owner who might want to go on to adjoining property to pick fruit that can not be reached from their own property.

## SECOND HAND INFORMATION

One of the worst situations is to be responding to a second hand or rumor complaint, particularly when dealing with a police matter. To often a resident will call the Association office and demand that staff call police on a traffic or civil disturbance matter. Staff or police do not want to talk to someone who has not observed the situation and can not provide first hand factual information. Residents have been very irritated when told that they should call the police directly because it was not appropriate for staff to call when they had not observed the problem. On numerous occasions I have responded to calls and gone to the site and found no problem. That is also why it may not be appropriate to respond to anonymous complaints. People do not want to get involved, but without their support, staff and the Association can be subject to abuse and claims of harassment.

## DON'T BECOME THE PERSONAL ENFORCER

When neighbors are feuding they would prefer to get the Association in the middle to become the enforcer. When feuding neighbors have been identified the enforcement process needs to be formalized with a paper trail that documents the complaints and the follow up. Our normal instinct is to be personal and helpful to residents with problems, but when residents attempt to use the Association for personal vendettas, a modified approach that is more formal with documentation is best.

## MEDIATION

Mediation is an excellent tool to not only resolve immediate problems but hopefully improve the relationship between neighbors. A manager or board member may be willing to play the role of mediator but only if both parties agree. Be sure to clarify the difference between mediation and arbitration. In mediation the role of the facilitator is to assist the parties in finding their own solution. In arbitration, the facilitator suggests solutions or in binding arbitration determines a final solution. A mediator must remain neutral and is not obligated to reach an equitable solution, but merely to help the participates reach a mutually acceptable solution.

*******

## CLOSING COMMENTS

This book has outlined several factors that may be considered when purchasing a home or investment property where there is a Homeowners' Association involved. This information is based on many years of experience as an on-site HOA manager as well as being an active Realtor. Although HOA professionals are generally referred to as property managers, the "people" aspect of HOA management is often the most challenging and may impact the reputation and livability of a property. The maintenance and management of common area is not rocket science, and more challenging can be dissent groups within associations creating conflict or negative publicity. The media has a history of exploiting sensationalized stories of unhappy homeowners, often distorting the facts or not providing a neutral presentation of both sides of the situation. Surveys by the national Community Association Institute (CAI) continues to show that the overwhelming majority of HOA members are happy homeowners and support their associations.

Although it is important that buyers evaluate the issues previously covered, often the final choice will be made based on the life style desired or location of the potential property. The desire to have such amenities as a view, beach access, participation in a resort or retirement community may require being in a Homeowners' Association. Once the decision has been made, competing developments need to be evaluated to find the property that not only meets the individual's desires, but has long range affordability for the potential buyer.

The objective of this book has not only been to assist a buyer in finding the best property, but to provide an understanding of how an HOA operates so a member can be an active participant.

Being an HOA member is not an end, but should be a continuing process with positive involvement to help the HOA be successful. Involvement may only mean passive support for the association or it could be a more positive experience by volunteering to serve on a committee or even running for the Board of Directors.

The internet can be a source of information on specific associations, many of which have web sites. Verify that the web site is being maintained by the association because often a real estate firm has obtained the domain name for promotional purposes or it may also be a site tainted by dissent groups or attorneys.

There are several professional groups that provide publications and educational material for HOAs. The national Community Association Institute (CAI) is an educational organization serving HOAs and their staffs. The CAI internet address is: www.caionline. org. There are CAI chapters in many states. The Institute of Real Estate Management (IREM) is a national association for real estate professionals, with chapters in many states and may be contacted at: www.irem.org. The Community Managers International Association (CMIA) represents large scale, on site community managers and may be contacted at: www.cmiamanager.org. There are also individual state associations, one of the largest being the California Association of Community Manager (CACM) which serves professional managers and may be contacted at: www.cacm. org. The Executive Council of Homeowners (ECHO) is a California based association of HOA Boards of Directors and may be contacted at: www.echo-ca.org. Web searches under "Homeowner Associations, Common Interest Developments, or Community Associations" will list a variety of web sites. Some of the referrals are attorneys and dissent groups or individuals, so the sources of any information should be carefully evaluated.

This book has not listed any reference publications because none were used. The information presented has generally been based on my experience as an on-site association manager and participation in the professional organizations listed in the previous paragraph.

Happy house hunting.

# GLOSSARY

**Annual Membership Meeting** – Association members meet to transact business and conduct elections.

**Alternate Dispute Resolution (ADR)** – An alternative to litigation to resolve disputes through mediation or arbitration.

**Association** – An organization of members for a common purpose, a Homeowners Association (HOA).

**Arbitration** – Settlement of a dispute by a neutral party.

**Architectural Committee (AC)** – An HOA Committee to process and enforce property modification rules.

**Articles of Incorporation** – Establishes a non-profit HOA and its purpose, structure and powers.

**Assessments** – Billing to HOA property owners to pay their share of expenses.

**Board of Directors** – Elected governing body of an HOA.

**Business Judgment Rule** – A standard of conduct for the governing body in conducting HOA business.

**By-Laws** – Establishes operating rules for an HOA.

**California Association of Community Managers (CACM)** – A California professional manager's organization.

**Certified Property Manager (CPM)** – A professional designation from the Institute of Real Management.

**Common Interest Development (CID)** – Community with shared common area facilities, such as condominiums, cooperatives and planned unit developments.

**Community Associations Institute (CAI)** – A non profit research and educational organization serving Homeowner Associations.

**Community Managers International Association (CMIA)** – A national on-site manager's professional managers association.

**Condominium** – A form of property ownership that combines exclusive use of a dwelling unit with shared ownership and use of common area.

**Cooperative (Co-op)** – Corporation ownership of an entire property with the residents being stock holders with the rights to occupy a specific unit.

**Corporation Code** – State Law applicable to corporations

**Covenants, Conditions & Restrictions (CC&Rs)** – Recorded documents detailing each owner's property rights and obligations in an HOA.

**Declaration of Limitations** – Recorded HOA document, also referred to as CC&Rs.

**Directors & Officers (D&O) Insurance** – Shield against losses arising out of actions of the Board of Directors in carrying out their prescribed duties.

**Executive Session** – A closed meeting of the Board of Directors to handle confidential or privacy issues.

**Fiduciaries** – Operating with the highest degree of trust in conducting business.

**General Membership** – Includes all members of an Association to conduct business.

**Homeowners Association (HOA)** – The organization of owners as a managing entity to conduct the business of maintaining and operating common property.

**Institute of Real Estate Management (IREM)** – A national professional organization serving property management by real estate agents.

**Mediation** – An alternative to litigation for settling disputes by using a neutral party during negotiations.

**Non Profit Mutual Benefit Corporation** – A type of Homeowner Association incorporation.

**Planned Unit Development (PUD)** – A form of ownership that may have individual titles to each parcel with joint ownership of common areas.

**Property Owners Association (POA)** – A similar title to a Homeowners Association (HOA).

**Quorum** – The number of members in attendance in person of by proxy needed to conduct business.

**Reserve Fund** – Funds set aside for long term repairs or replacement of major common area facilities or major components.

**Special Assessment** – An unanticipated fee levied against members for unexpected expenses.

**Townhouse** – A type of condominium unit that does not have a unit above or below and may include title to the land under the unit.

# ABOUT THE AUTHOR:

CLAUDE JOHN "CJ" KLUG has been involved in Homeowner Associations for over 25 years and served as an on-site manager of several large Associations with a variety of amenities, including golf courses and retirement communities. Associations managed include: Coto de Caza, Casta Del Sol, Niguel Shores, Nellie Gail Ranch and Palm Desert Greens. He has also served on HOA Boards of Directors and been a consultant to Real Estate Developers and HOA Boards.

As a former member of the national Community Associations Institute, including service as Chapter President, he authored articles for national and chapter publications and received the Professional Community Association Manager designation. He was a founding member of the California Association of Community Managers and served on the Board of Directors and Professional Standards Committee. He was also a founding member of the Community Managers International Association, served on the Board of Directors and received the Master Community Manager designation.

Prior to working with Homeowner Associations, he spent 25 years in City Management and Redevelopment, with the following California Cities: La Mirada, Commerce, Pasadena, Garden Grove and Pico Rivera.

Mr. Klug has B.A. and M.A. degrees from California State University at Long Beach. He currently resides in Honolulu, Hawaii, and can be contacted by email at: Mgroncall@msn.com.

*HOMEOWNERS ASSOCIATIONS, What you should know before buying in an HOA, and how to become an effective HOA member.*

DISCAIMER: The materials presented are the generalized opinions of the author and each Association may have unique CC&Rs and be located in States with different governmental or corporate laws. The material presented in this book is not intended to be a substitution for consulting with appropriate legal counsel or other professional advisors.